The Nintendo Wii
PocketGuide

Bart G. **Farkas**

*All the Secrets of the Nintendo Wii,
Pocket Sized.*

**Peachpit
Press**

The Nintendo Wii Pocket Guide

Bart G. Farkas

Peachpit Press
1249 Eighth Street
Berkeley, CA 94710
510/524-2178
510/524-2221 (fax)

Find us on the Web at: www.peachpit.com
To report errors, please send a note to errata@peachpit.com

Peachpit Press is a division of Pearson Education.

Editors: Clifford Colby and Kathy Simpson
Production editor: Hilal Sala
Compositor: David Van Ness
Indexer: Rebecca Plunkett
Cover design and photography: Aren Howell
Interior design: Kim Scott, with Maureen Forys

ISBN-13: 978-0-321-51011-2
ISBN-10:   0-321-51011-9

9 8 7 6 5 4 3 2 1

Printed and bound in the United States of America

Dedication

For my family

Acknowledgments

As with any book of this sort, I have plenty of people to thank. First off, Kathy Simpson deserves a huge thank-you for her fine editing work, pointing out logic problems and turning the raw text into something readable. Cliff Colby deserves similar credit. Without Cliff, the book wouldn't fly—and that point is clearly demonstrated in Chapter 4, in which a Mii is created in his honor.

It's also important for me to thank the folks at Engadget and Benjamin Heckendorn, who allowed us to use a picture of his Wii Laptop creation.

Despite the fact that my kids are constant distractions and thorns in my side, their contributions to this book were invaluable. From my littlest one (Natasha, who's 3) to my oldest (Adam, who's 8), they all contributed a great deal in helping me figure out the nuances of the Wii.

My better half, Cori, is always a help during the writing of a book. Even she had to admit (grudgingly) that the Everybody Votes Channel is a nice way of bringing the family together so that we can discuss our opinions about the various questions asked and then see how our ideas compare with the rest of the world's.

Contents

Chapter 1: The Wii Arrives 1

Before the Wii... 2

What Makes the Wii Different? 4
The controllers 4
Virtual Console 11
Miis and the Wii Community 12

A Tour of the Wii Interface 14

Chapter 2: Wii: Out of the Box.................. 19

What Comes with the Wii? 20

The Ins and Outs of the Wii.............................. 22
Cables and spaces 24
Remotes..25
Stands...26
Included software: Wii Sports...........................27

The Guts of the Wii....................................... 30
Processor...30
Storage...31
Ports 33
Audio and video capabilities...........................33

Setting up the Wii.. 34
Setting up the Wii Remote...........................36
Connecting to the Internet...........................39

Chapter 3: The Channels...................... 47

Disc Channel... 48

Mii Channel 51
Hanging with the Miis.................................52
Creating and editing Miis..............................54

Photo Channel 55
   Photo views 56
   Other photo fun 61

Wii Shop Channel 65
   Wii Ware 65
   Virtual Console 66

Forecast Channel 67

News Channel 69
   Viewing news items 69
   Highlighting text 70

Everybody Votes Channel 72

Internet Channel 74

Chapter 4: Mii and You 77

Why Mii? 78

Making a Mii 79
   Where to start 80
   Building your Mii 81

Navigating Mii Plaza 91

Managing Miis 93
   Zooming 93
   Grabbing Miis 94
   Arranging Miis 95
   Sending a Mii to a friend 96
   Transferring Miis 98

Editing Miis Outside the Wii 100
   Web-based editors 100
   PC-based editors 104

Chapter 5: Wii Controllers 107

The Wii Remote 108
What makes the Wii Remote tick? 109
How does the Wii Remote communicate? 111
Settings 114
Calibration 114

Chapter 6: Beyond Gaming 119

The Wii As Internet Appliance 120
Getting connected 120
Surfing the Web 124
Setting parental controls 127
Wii-mailing 131

Wii Belong 132
Memos 132
Calendar 132

Chapter 7: Shopping: It's What Wii Do 135

Shopping the Wii Shop Channel 137
Using Wii Points Cards 137
Making a Virtual Console purchase 144
Buying Wii Ware 149

Shopping on the Internet 151

Chapter 8: A-Gaming Wii Will Go 153

What to Look for in a Wii Game 154

The Best Wii Games 157
GT Pro Series 158
The Legend of Zelda: Twilight Princess 159
Madden NFL 07 160
Rayman Raving Rabbids 161

Red Steel 162
Wario Ware: Smooth Moves. 163

Backward Compatibility. 164
Virtual Console 165
GameCube games 169

Chapter 9: Wii Accessories. 173

Protection and Beauty. 174
Skins 174
Wrist straps 176

Functional Accessories 176
Intec G5615 Wii Vertical Stand 176
Intec Wii Pro Gamer's Case. 178
Nintendo Component AV cable 179
Battery chargers 181
Nintendo Wi-Fi USB Connector 182
Nintendo Wii LAN Adapter 182
Wii Sports Pack controller adapters 183
Ubisoft Wii steering wheel 184

SD Cards 184

Chapter 10: Wii Mods and Hacks. 189

Wii Console Hacks 190
Copy-related mods. 191
Wii software mods 195
Mii modifications. 198

Wii Remote Hacks. 205
Windows and the Wii Remote 205
Other uses for the remote. 206

Index 209

1

The Wii Arrives

The holiday season of 2006 was not unlike most other holiday seasons, in that there tended to be chaos at shopping malls, in parking lots, and (no doubt) in more than a few homes. In December, one gift captured the imagination of the country—indeed, the continent—and that was the Nintendo Wii.

A rather odd device as current gaming consoles go, with its wireless controllers and simple yet engrossing games and interface, the Wii attracted young and old alike, generating a raging fire of enthusiasm and demand.

In fact, the Wii (*Wii* is pronounced "we") is causing a paradigm shift in the gaming community. (I hate using the term *paradigm shift,* but in this case, I can't think of a better choice of words.) This gaming system brings people and gamers together in groups that can best be described as families or communities, often encouraging them to communicate in physically expressive ways. The Wii fits into family activities in a way that parents can be enthusiastic about. From good old-fashioned fun to weight-loss activities, the Wii is changing the face of gaming and opening a gateway to the online world that is as accessible for the 8-year-old as it is for the 80-year-old.

Before the Wii

Started in Japan way back in 1889, Nintendo made its way by creating handmade playing-card games for many years. By the 1960s, Nintendo had branched out into hotels, food, and even television networks. Unfortunately for the company, none of these ventures ended up being particularly successful. In the early 1980s, Nintendo released a videogame called Donkey Kong for the Atari 2600, Intellivision, and ColecoVision consoles—and the modern company we know was born.

With its huge success in the gaming software market, Nintendo decided to take the plunge into hardware, and in the middle 1980s, the Nintendo Entertainment System (NES) hit the market. The results were immediate and long lasting. With the

NES, Nintendo had a proprietary platform for which it could grow its own games and characters.

In 1989, the Nintendo Game Boy—the first ultrasuccessful handheld gaming platform—hit the market, followed by the Super Nintendo Entertainment System (SNES) in 1991. In the mid-1990s, the Nintendo 64 (N64) ushered in the era of consoles worth buying just for the games that come with them. The N64 came with Super Mario 64, a fantastic platform game that is still a technological marvel.

In an attempt to keep up with Sony's PlayStation 2, the Sega Dreamcast, and the then-new Xbox from Microsoft, Nintendo came out with the GameCube in 2001. Nintendo has sold more than 21 million GameCubes, but even with those numbers, it hasn't kept up with Sony in terms of raw sales. Still, the GameCube was (and still is) a success, with the standard Mario and Zelda games taking full advantage of the console's processing power.

That brings us to today—and the Wii. When Nintendo released it in November 2006, the Wii was the runaway hit of the holiday season—the product that everyone wanted but few could get. Many would-be buyers lined up outside stores for hours only to be disappointed. Even as I write this book, Nintendo is struggling to meet demand for the diminutive device. In fact, in February 2007 Merrill Lynch predicted that 30 percent of all U.S. homes will have a Wii by 2011. That prediction may or may not come to fruition. Still, Merrill Lynch usually does its homework (and that's no bull!).

What Makes the Wii Different?

The Wii is a departure from all of Nintendo's other consoles in several respects:

- The controllers are wireless and motion sensitive.

- Although it's small and not based on cutting-edge technology, the Wii gets the absolute maximum out of what Nintendo gave it.

- The Wii has built-in Internet connectivity.

- The Wii is backward compatible with GameCube games, giving GameCube owners an incentive to upgrade to the Wii.

The following sections cover some of the features that make the Wii stand out in the crowd.

The controllers

Control of the Wii goes through one device: the Wii Remote. When it comes to Wii-specific software and games, you *must* have a Wii Remote as a starting point; otherwise, you won't be doing anything. All other controllers connect to the Wii Remote—with the exception of GameCube controllers, which have their own (wired) connector slots. Still, to start a GameCube game, you need your handy-dandy Wii Remote.

Wii Remote

The standard Wii controller, known as the *Wii Remote* (**Figure 1.1**), is at the heart of the Wii's innovative feel. This controller looks much like an average television remote control, only it's a little bit thicker and more square than streamlined. Despite its slightly chunky shape, the Wii Remote has a surprisingly comfortable feel, making it intuitive and easy to use.

Figure 1.1
The main controller—the Wii Remote—is a thing of beauty.

By taking advantage of coordinated inputs from a Bluetooth wireless connection, infrared beams, and internal accelerometers, the Wii Remote communicates with the Wii's external sensor bar (**Figure 1.2**), which sits either on top of or below your television set. With this unique wireless setup, the Wii can sense the controller's exact position in three-dimensional space, allowing a plethora of actions—from swinging a golf club to balancing a tray of cocktail drinks.

Figure 1.2
The external sensor bar makes the Wii Remote work wonderfully.

Another feature that makes the Wii Remote special is its built-in memory, which allows you to copy and save Mii characters—custom-made in-game people—directly to the remote. (Miis are covered later in this chapter and in Chapter 4.)

Indeed, you can use the Wii Remote to transfer Miis from one Wii unit to another. The remote also contains force feedback, which adds greatly to the feel of every movement, from moving your cursor over a button to getting bumped off the road in a virtual race car.

Finally, the remote has a speaker that provides little auditory responses to onscreen actions, both in the standard Wii menu and in the games and other software. Hearing a sound when a button is clicked or an action occurs adds greatly to the Wii experience. It may not seem like much, but you can't underestimate the added spice that sound and tactile feedback provide.

Safety First: Use the Wrist Strap

Each Wii Remote comes with a wrist strap that's designed to keep the user from throwing the remote during particularly active in-game movements. In Wii Sports Boxing, for example, the idea is to punch toward the TV (actually, the Wii sensor bar) hard and fast. If you're not using the wrist strap, and your grip lapses during a punch, the Nunchuk might fly toward the TV and put a nice hole in it. For this reason, I recommend (and so does Nintendo) that you *always* use your wrist strap, no matter what you are using the Wii or the Wii Remote for.

A few recent lawsuits have claimed that overexuberant game play caused the wrist straps to break, thereby sending Wii Remotes careening into other areas of users' houses. My independent studies show that it's highly unlikely for a person to break the strap and send the remote spiraling out of control. Even if you exert enough force to break the strap, the remote usually won't travel more than a few inches in any direction before it hits the floor.

The Nunchuk

The Nunchuk (**Figure 1.3**) is an add-on controller—
meaning that it plugs into the bottom of the Wii
Remote and cannot connect to the Wii console
directly. This device is used in certain games (such as
Rayman Raving Rabbids and Wii Sports Boxing) as
the off-hand controller. The Nunchuk features a two-
button Control Stick and an accelerometer, which
lets you use the Nunchuk in conjunction with the Wii
Remote to control games with both hands.

Figure 1.3
The Nunchuk
add-on
controller for
the Wii Remote.

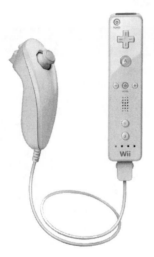

Some games, such as Red Steel from Ubisoft, use the
Nunchuk as a movement device (the Control Stick)
and the Wii Remote as the pointing or "looking"
device. If you have a Wii, a Nunchuk is a must-have
for many games.

Classic Controller

The Classic Controller (**Figure 1.4**), like the Nunchuk, connects directly to the Wii Remote, but it mirrors the remote control of the Nintendo GameCube or SNES sufficiently that you can use it to play older games on the Virtual Console (covered later in this chapter and in Chapters 5 and 7). Although you can use GameCube controllers for the same purposes, the Classic Controller is an excellent controller for all the simple games that are downloadable via the Wii Shop Channel (covered in Chapter 7) and for certain GameCube games.

Figure 1.4
You can use the Classic Controller for GameCube and Virtual Console games.

GameCube controllers

One beautiful thing about the Wii is that it's backward compatible with the Nintendo GameCube. Being backward compatible is all well and good, but how on earth (you may ask) are you supposed to play GameCube games with the Wii controllers? The answer is, quite simply, you're not!

Well, that's not entirely true, because the Classic Controller can indeed do the job, but the Wii contains four GameCube controller slots as well as two memory slots for GameCube memory cards. In short, the Wii is a fully functional GameCube with built-in Wii capabilities. So go ahead and use your old GameCube Controller (**Figure 1.5**) to play your GameCube games.

Figure 1.5
The venerable GameCube controllers are still useful on the Wii.

tip As a bonus, most Virtual Console games that require the Classic Controller can be handled entirely with a GameCube controller if you happen to have one plugged into your Wii.

Virtual Console

Another great thing about the Wii is that it can play older games created for the Sega Genesis, the TurboGrafx, the NES, the SNES, and the N64. These games are available via the Wii Shop Channel in the Virtual Console (**Figure 1.6**); they are not particularly expensive, and the list of titles is growing. This capability is a great way to play some all-time classic games without having to dig out your old systems and buy the old game cartridges from eBay.

Figure 1.6
The Wii Shop
Channel in the
Virtual Console.

Miis and the Wii Community

Miis (**Figure 1.7**) are little personalized characters that you create in the Mii Channel (covered in Chapter 4). Miis walk around in Mii Plaza or march in Mii Parades. They're also used as characters in most games, and game scores are attached to particular Miis.

Figure 1.7
An assortment of Miis—one of which is me.

When you're in the Mii Channel, you can create your own individual Mii (**Figure 1.8**), specifying eye color and shape, hair color and style, face shape and color, body size, and many other parameters.

Figure 1.8
Creating a Mii
is a blast.

Your Mii is an extension of your personality that you can send, via Wii Mail, to other Wii users who are connected to the Internet; it can also travel to other Wii systems that you don't know about. Likewise, other Mii characters are bound to show up on your Wii, and you can accept them into your Mii Plaza (or not).

Miis add a great deal to the experience on the Wii, so creating at least one avatar is well worth your while.

What Is an Avatar?

An *avatar* is a representation of a person in Internet-related activities. Avatars vary between simple 2D images and complex 3D representations. People sometimes choose avatars that represent what they actually look like; others choose avatars that are what they *want* to look like. Either way, avatars are very popular ways for people to express themselves in online communities.

A Tour of the Wii Interface

Chapter 3 examines the Wii's interface in detail, but because the interface is part of what makes the Wii so compelling and useful, it's worth mentioning here as well.

The main interface of the Wii is a panel of screens—12 screens in one panel—that individually look like miniature TV screens. These small screens are called *channels,* with each channel offering either a set of services or a particular game or piece of software (**Figure 1.9**).

Figure 1.9
Each little "TV screen" represents a game or a specific area of the Wii universe.

The channel in the top-left corner of the main interface is the Disc Channel (**Figure 1.10**), which is the place to go to fire up GameCube games, Wii games, or other software that comes on disc (be it a 12-inch or a 5-inch disc).

Figure 1.10
The Disc Channel shows you what discs are options in your machine.

The other channels can contain games or software obtained from the Wii Shop Channel, but the Wii has several standard channels:

- Disc Channel

- Wii Shop Channel

- News Channel (updated Wii only)

- Everybody Votes Channel (updated Wii only)

- Forecast Channel

- Photo Channel

- Internet Channel (updated Wii only)

note Some channels require you to update your Wii before you can use or access them. I'm not exactly sure why that is, but if you want to enjoy these channels, you must commit to the updates. When you try to access one of these channels, the Wii displays a dialog box that offers you the updates; click OK to get them.

The two controls in the main interface are the Wii Settings button, in the bottom-left corner, and the Mail button, in the bottom-right corner. The Settings button takes you to the Wii's basic settings and parameters (**Figure 1.11**), such as language, parental controls, and system settings. The Mail button takes you to a screen where you can compose and send mail to friends, set up tasks in a calendar, and make notes for yourself. The main interface is very easy to use, and it's a joy to navigate.

Figure 1.11
The Wii Settings screen.

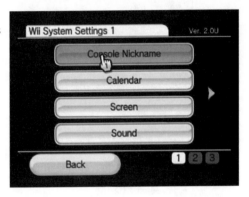

Test-Driving the Wii

Back when the Wii was first being displayed for industry insiders at E3 (the Electronic Entertainment Expo) in Los Angeles, I had a chance to see the Wii in action and use it firsthand. Unfortunately, the line to use a Wii for a few short minutes stretched all the way around the Nintendo booth (quite a large area), and frankly, I wasn't particularly interested in spending my time standing in such a long line for a payoff that lasted only a couple of minutes.

I'll be honest—the buzz about the Wii at the beginning of the show wasn't particularly strong. My crowd of contemporaries was more interested in two other upcoming platforms: the Xbox 360 and the PlayStation 3. Some of my colleagues, however, were interested enough to spend 45 minutes in line waiting for the chance to see the Wii. What they had to say about the Wii when they returned wasn't what I was expecting to hear. "It's pretty cool; the wireless remote is really impressive," one of my most trusted companions said.

As the show wore on, the word continued to filter out: The Wii was not a joke. I was a tad surprised, because it seemed to me that Nintendo was losing touch with the gaming community, making some rather odd decisions that played negatively with the gaming crowd.

Fast-forward to the Wii's release. A few of my close friends purchased the Wii and told me how great it is. I gave in and (after quite a bit of searching) managed to track down a Wii in another province. On Christmas morning, I made the Wii the final gift that my kids received, and they were very excited. We broke open the box, plugged it in, connected it to the TV, and inserted the Wii Sports disc that came with the unit. Within 10 minutes, my 8-year-old son Adam and I were pulverizing each other in a round of virtual boxing, jabbing left and right, dodging back and forth, and generally throwing furious punches in an attempt to knock each other out.

(continues on next page)

Test-Driving the Wii (continued)

After 7 or 8 minutes, the boxing match was over, and I emerged the victor (something that I almost never do anymore). But something else had occurred: I was dripping with sweat and felt unusually exhilarated, having enjoyed the brief match with my son more than any recent gaming experience.

From boxing, we moved on to a round of bowling, this time including my younger son, Derek, in the game. Then we had a go at three holes of golf, with Dad again coming in first but all three of us enjoying the experience immensely.

The last game Adam and I tried was baseball, in which the pitcher actually winds up and feigns throwing the Wii Remote while the batter holds his or her remote like a baseball bat, swinging as the pitch arrives. The game ended in a scoreless tie after three innings, but despite the lack of scoring, everyone in the room had the same reaction: "This is awesome!"

The Wii has much more to offer than just the one game that comes with it, of course, but on Christmas Day 2006, it became abundantly clear to me that the Wii is a different type of device. It's not only a gaming machine with a new input medium, but also an Internet appliance that's capable of bringing families, friends, and even strangers closer together.

2

Wii: Out of the Box

The Wii is packaged in a relatively small box, but it comes with everything you need to enjoy it as a single-user appliance. For those folks who want to take full advantage of the Wii's gaming prowess, some accessories have to be on the "to acquire" list. Otherwise, not much two-player action will happen; the Wii will be a solitary endeavor.

To help you decide whether you need to purchase anything to go with your first Wii, this chapter looks at what's inside each Wii box, examining the features and the guts of the Wii so that you can see what this machine can do. Then I'll show you how to set it up and how to connect to the Internet in the quickest, most efficient manner.

note

I use the word *appliance* because the Wii is much more than just a gaming machine. It is in fact an Internet appliance that lets users send and receive email, surf the Internet, shop, manage photos, receive key information such as weather and news, and generally connect to the world as a whole.

What Comes with the Wii?

The Wii comes with everything you need to get started for a single-user situation (**Figure 2.1**). But like all consoles on the market, the basic kit lacks a second controller (in this case, a second Wii Remote), which makes dual-user capability possible only when the users can hand one remote back and forth.

Figure 2.1
A Wii stands ready in its brilliant white packaging.

Here's exactly what comes with the Wii right out of the box:

- Wii console

- Wii Remote

- Nunchuk controller

- Vertical stand and plate

- Sensor bar and stand

- AC adapter

- AV cable

- Wii Sports disc

- Wii Operations Manual and other documentation

The Ins and Outs of the Wii

The Wii console contains a series of buttons as well as two doors that give you access to the GameCube portion of the Wii and the SD Memory Card access slot for the Wii. **Figure 2.2, Figure 2.3,** and **Figure 2.4** also show where the power adapter, the AV adapter, the sensor bar, and the USB connectors are located.

Power button

Power LED

Reset

Sync button

SD card slot

Game disc slot

Eject button

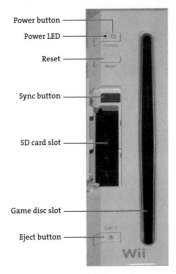

Figure 2.2
Front view of
the Wii.

Figure 2.3
Back view of
the Wii.

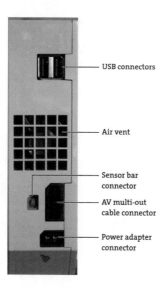

USB connectors

Air vent

Sensor bar
connector

AV multi-out
cable connector

Power adapter
connector

GameCube
memory-card slots   GameCube controller sockets

A   B   4   3   2   1

Figure 2.4
Top view of
the Wii.

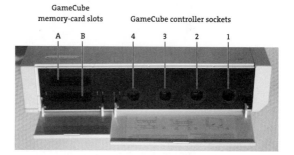

Cables and spaces

The basic AV cable (**Figure 2.5**) and the AC power cable for the Wii (**Figure 2.6**) are self-explanatory in terms of where you attach them on the Wii and how you plug them into a power outlet or the inputs on a television.

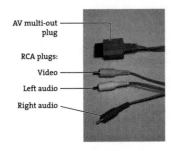

AV multi-out plug

RCA plugs:
Video
Left audio
Right audio

DC plug AC plug

Figure 2.5
The Wii's AV cable.

Figure 2.6
The power cable included with the Wii.

What's perhaps most impressive about the Wii is that it's essentially a GameCube and a Wii all in one. Flip up the cover on the top of the Wii, and you see the GameCube area, which contains four GameCube controller sockets and two GameCube memory-card slots.

The small door on the front of the Wii gives you access to the Sync button (which you use to synchronize Wii Remotes with this particular Wii) and the SD card slot, which allows you to add storage space to your Wii via an SD (secure digital) Memory Card.

Remotes

The Wii Remote and the Nunchuk are the two input devices that come with the Wii.

The Wii Remote (**Figure 2.7**) is the backbone input device, working entirely wirelessly—indeed, seemingly magically. It contains accelerometers, infrared sensors, a speaker, and a vibrating feedback mechanism that causes the remote to actually jolt in your hand in concert with what's happening onscreen.

Figure 2.7
The Wii Remote.

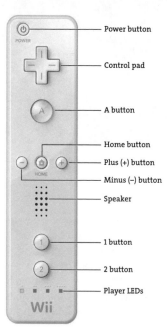

Power button

Control pad

A button

Home button

Plus (+) button

Minus (–) button

Speaker

1 button

2 button

Player LEDs

The Nunchuk (**Figure 2.8**) is reserved for gaming applications, but because it's required for Wii Boxing (included in Wii Sports), the folks at Nintendo made sure that it's part of the basic Wii kit. Although it too contains such things as accelerometers, the Nunchuk works only when hooked to a Wii Remote via the connector at the base of the device.

Figure 2.8
The Nunchuk control.

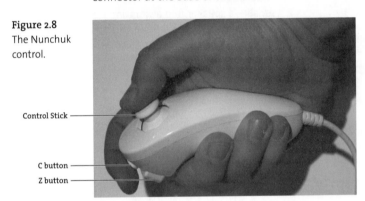

Control Stick

C button
Z button

Stands

You can set up the Wii in a horizontal configuration or in a vertical fashion to save space and (arguably) to look more hip. The vertical stand that comes with the Wii allows you to set the console on its end with more confidence. The stand plate adds stability to the vertical configuration so that you're less likely (or at least relatively less likely) to pull the Wii off its perch during a game that involves a GameCube controller connected to the Wii by a wire.

Included software: Wii Sports

Besides the operating system that is built into the device, the Wii comes with Wii Sports, an ingenious collection of sports games that takes advantage of the wireless Wii Remote and provides instant enjoyment. The Wii Sports disc includes these games:

- **Tennis.** For new Wii users, Tennis seems to be the most difficult game to get the hang of.

- **Golf.** The Wii's three-hole Golf game is lots of fun. It demonstrates the power of the Wii Remote to act like anything, including a golf club.

- **Bowling.** Fun for the whole family, Bowling requires little skill and can be played by anyone between the ages of 4 and 100.

- **Baseball.** Baseball is three innings of fun in which pitching and batting are the entire object; fielding is automatic. The players switch from batting to pitching at the top and bottom of each inning.

- **Boxing.** The most dramatic of the Wii Sports games, Boxing pits two boxers against each other in a three-round bout.

Of the Wii Sports games, Boxing (**Figure 2.9**) is the one that most kids want to play immediately. After you play even one round, you quickly realize that the Wii has the capability to do something besides just entertain and serve as an Internet appliance; it can also be used very effectively as exercise equipment. You heard me correctly: The Wii is actually a tool for helping people stay active and lose weight. (More on that later.)

Figure 2.9
Wii Sports Boxing is a workout, both mentally and physically.

note In Boxing, you need the Nunchuk so that both of the boxer's hands can register punches or evasive maneuvers.

Pretty much all the games are more enjoyable when played by two people, but the lack of a second controller can be an obstacle. Fortunately, two people can play Bowling and Golf merely by swapping the Wii Remote. Still, the real joy of Baseball, Boxing, and Tennis comes when two Wii Remotes are available so that two players can truly go head to head.

Boxing with the Amazing Wii Remote

When you take a stab at Wii Sports Boxing, you really begin to see the power of the Wii and its wireless remote system. The Wii Remote and Nunchuk enable you to throw specific punches with both hands, your onscreen persona throwing the same punches that your offscreen body is throwing in midair (**Figure 2.10**). But the remote and Nunchuk also sense when your body moves from side to side, and the onscreen boxer you are controlling moves from side to side with you. Add to this the fact that the remote gives you physical feedback in the form of a jolt—as well as auditory feedback—every time you get hit by your opponent or land a particularly solid punch, and you've got a control system that changes the way games are played.

Figure 2.10
Derek and Adam (the author's sons) fight it out in Wii Sports Boxing, each holding a Wii Remote and a Nunchuk.

The result is a round of boxing that's remarkably like a real-world match, with the opponents dodging left and right; throwing jabs, roundabouts, and uppercuts; and generally looking like real boxers. Even though the players aren't facing each other—they're standing side by side facing a TV set—they are nonetheless engaged in what they perceive to be a battle of pugilistic honor. The effect is a lot of fun and surprisingly healthy. Indeed, the first time I played Wii Sports Boxing against my 8-year-old son Adam, I managed to record a victory, but at the end of three rounds I was also pouring sweat, and my heart rate was up considerably.

The Guts of the Wii

The Wii is a powerful gaming console, but perhaps the most surprising aspect of this new gaming system is that it really can't compete with Microsoft's Xbox 360 or Sony's PlayStation 3 in terms of raw computing power or graphical capabilities. Nintendo obviously made a conscious choice to create a unit that, although impressive, is not intended to set the gaming world on fire with its power. Indeed, the company went after the gaming market with a plan to create an adequate, inexpensive, yet paradigm-creating console that incorporated existing technology in ways that would make it irresistible to gamers and families alike.

This strategy paid off in spades, because the Wii continues to be a hot item. Even as I write this paragraph, months after the holiday season of 2006–07, the Wii is still sold out at every store in my area, and a scan of the major online retailers, such as Best Buy, tells much the same story.

The following sections examine the technical aspects of the Wii.

Processor

The processors are the real guts of a console's (or any computer's) performance. Generally speaking, a gaming console such as the Wii has a central processing unit (CPU) and a visual processing unit (also known as a graphics processing unit, or GPU), and from these two units, the console derives its power.

- The CPU is a PowerPC "Broadway" processor that runs at 729 MHz.

- The GPU is an ATI "Hollywood" processor that runs near 250 MHz.

Computers and videogame consoles with separate video processors are relatively recent developments. For many years, the graphics on a computer were managed by a built-in graphics chip or—heaven forbid—by the computer's own CPU. As consumer demand for more detailed, impressive animations and graphics increased, so did the need for more powerful graphics chips. Today, it's not uncommon for a person buying and assembling a new computer for gaming purposes to spend more money on the video processor than on the computer's main CPU.

Storage

The Wii comes with built-in flash memory for storing downloads and other important information (such as saved games), but it also includes an expansion slot for an SD Memory Card. The GameCube area of the Wii contains slots for GameCube memory cards, and the disc drive can handle both the 12-cm Wii optical discs and the 8-cm GameCube discs.

The Wii Remote also has an important storage feature. Each remote has a small amount of memory (only 6 KB) that you can use to store as many as 10 Mii characters. This feature allows you to back up special Mii characters or transfer Mii characters to a friend's system with ease.

The Wii's storage features are as follows:

- 512 MB built-in flash memory

- Single SD Memory Card slot

- Two GameCube memory-card slots

- Slot-loading optical disc drive for GameCube and Wii discs (read-only)

- 6 KB EPROM (Erasable Programmable Read-Only Memory) in the Wii Remote

note SD Memory Cards come in several flavors, from 256 MB up to 4 GB. For this book, I bought two 1 GB SD cards to store saved games and downloaded Virtual Console titles. A 1 GB SD card currently runs about $29. When I consider that I once spent $499 on a 16 KB memory upgrade for my Commodore Vic 20 computer, it boggles my mind to imagine that I can now spend 1/17th as much for a memory chip that's roughly 64,000 times larger (in terms of storage) and about 1/100th the size of the 16 KB memory upgrade.

Ports

Outlets include the actual ports, peripheral connections, and adapter-connection locations on the Wii. Following are all the ports on the Wii:

- Four GameCube controller ports

- One SD Memory Card slot

- Two GameCube memory-card slots

- Sensor bar port

- AC adapter port

- AV cable port

- Two USB 2.0 ports

- Internal 802.11 b/g wireless module for Wi-Fi Internet connection

Audio and video capabilities

This section looks at the capabilities of the Wii's basic output in terms of video and audio output:

- For video, the Wii is capable of standard NTSC output or 480p progressive-scan output.

- Video can be connected via RGB, S-Video, or Component connectors.

- Audio output is stereo, with Dolby Pro Logic II capability.

- Audio output in the controller is via a single built-in speaker.

Setting up the Wii

You fought off the crowds at the stores, bribed the clerk, acquired a Wii, and got it to your house without anyone ripping it out of your hands along the way. Now what do you do? The answer is simple: You set up the Wii and get the ball rolling with your brand-new and exciting gaming console.

To set up your Wii, follow these steps:

1. Remove the Wii from its box.

2. Remove the AC adapter and the AV cable from their packaging.

3. Remove the vertical stand, stand plate, sensor bar, and sensor-bar stand from their packaging.

4. Remove the Wii Remote and Nunchuk from their packaging.

5. Find a place near your TV for the Wii, and set up the Wii horizontally or vertically (**Figure 2.11**).

Figure 2.11
Depending on available space or maybe even aesthetics, you may want to place your Wii vertically instead of in the traditional horizontal position.

6. Connect the AC adapter and the AV cable to the Wii.

7. Plug the AC adapter into a power outlet, and connect the AV cable to the input on your TV, with the yellow cable going to the video input and the red and white cables going to the audio inputs.

8. Put the batteries in the remote control (**Figure 2.12**).

Figure 2.12
Your Wii Remote takes two AA batteries, which are included.

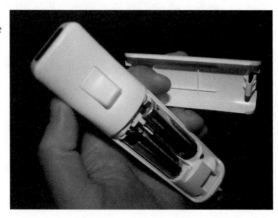

9. Turn on the Wii.

10. Follow the onscreen instructions to set a language, your location, time of day, and so on.

Setting up the Wii Remote

As gut-wrenchingly simple as the Wii is, it has a slight wrinkle when it comes to Wii Remotes. Wii Remotes don't bond to your Wii console automatically; they actually have to be told to do that.

The remote control that comes with your console is prebonded to it, but any extra Wii Remotes you may have purchased have to be synchronized with your Wii to work with the console smoothly. You can do this in two ways: One Time Mode and Standard Mode.

One Time Mode

One Time Mode allows your Wii Remote to work with a Wii other than the one it is synchronized with. If you go to a friend's house to play some Wii Golf, for example, and he has only one Wii Remote, you can take your remote along and synchronize it with your friend's Wii, using One Time Mode. Follow these steps:

1. Press the Home button on the Wii Remote that is already synchronized with the Wii console you want to use.

2. Select the Wii Remote Settings option; then select the Reconnect option (**Figure 2.13**).

Figure 2.13
Click the Wii
Remote Settings
option at the
bottom of the
screen to get to
the Reconnect
option.

3. After you click the Reconnect button onscreen
   with the Wii Remote's cursor, simultaneously
   (and physically) press the 1 and 2 buttons on the
   remote that you want to sync with the console.

   When the lights stop blinking and your remote
   vibrates slightly (you can feel it in your hand),
   your remote has synchronized temporarily with
   that Wii console. The attachment of the remote is
   reflected onscreen as well.

Standard Mode

Use Standard Mode to connect additional Wii
Remotes to your Wii system permanently—when
you've purchased (or otherwise acquired) new
remotes for your system, for example, and you want
to have them available for game play at all times.

To synchronize a new remote with your Wii, follow these steps:

1. Press the Power button on the Wii console to turn it on.

2. Remove the battery cover on the back of the Wii Remote, and press the Sync button inside the cover (**Figure 2.14**).

Figure 2.14
The LEDs on the front of the remote blink when you press the Sync button.

3. Open the door over the SD card slot on the Wii console, and press the Sync button inside that compartment (**Figure 2.15**).

When the LEDs on the remote stop blinking, synchronization is complete.

Figure 2.15
Press the red
Sync button just
inside the door
on the front of
the Wii.

Connecting to the Internet

Part of what makes the Wii special is its ability to
connect to the Internet with ease, giving you access
to the information and shopping channels that are
available only with an Internet connection. You can
connect the Wii to the Internet through wireless
connections or wired connections.

Connecting via an existing wireless network

To connect to the Internet via an existing wireless
connection in your house, office, or wherever you
are, you need only your Wii, a power source, and a
functional Wii Remote. Assuming that your wireless
network is not encrypted, you can connect with the
following method:

1. In the main Wii menu, move to the bottom-left corner and click the Wii Options button (**Figure 2.16**).

Figure 2.16
Click Wii
Options.

2. Click the Wii Settings button.

3. Move to the Wii System Settings 2 screen by clicking the arrow button; then click the Internet button (**Figure 2.17**).

Figure 2.17
The Internet
button is in
the Wii System
Settings 2
screen.

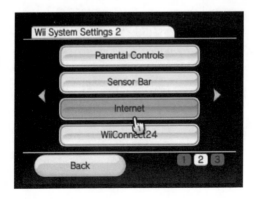

4. Click the Connection Settings button; then click the Wireless Connection button (**Figure 2.18**).

Figure 2.18
Click Wireless
Connection.

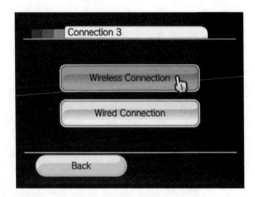

5. Click Search for an Access Point.

After you do this, the system searches for available wireless networks and lists them onscreen.

6. Select the network you want to use.

7. Click the Test Connection button to see whether your connection is working.

That's it!

If your wireless network is encrypted, use this procedure:

1. Complete steps 1 through 5 of the preceding list.

   After you click Search for an Access Point and select a network, the Wii displays a screen that asks for a key or password (**Figure 2.19**).

Figure 2.19
Here, the Wii needs a password to access an AirPort wireless network. Click the white box to get to the input screen.

2. In the input screen, enter the WEP key or password for your wireless network, and click OK (**Figure 2.20**).

   When the correct password or key is in place, the Wii is connected.

Figure 2.20
In this screen, enter your key or password to access an encrypted wireless network.

note

If you have access to an encrypted wireless network, no doubt you know the key or password for it, because your computer connects in the same way. Beyond telling you that you need to have this information, I can't help you further because of the nature of WEP (short for Wired Equivalent Privacy) encryption passwords, keys, and wireless systems; it's impossible to walk you through them all.

Connecting via a Nintendo Wi-Fi USB Connector

If you don't have an existing wireless connection nearby, but you *do* have a computer nearby that's connected to the Internet, you can use Nintendo's Wi-Fi USB Connector to turn your PC into a wireless broadcaster/receiver that your Wii can connect to.

To do this, first you need to complete steps 1 through 4 in "Connecting via an existing wireless network" earlier in this chapter. Then you need to move to your PC and install the software from the disc that comes with the USB connector, as follows:

1. Insert the USB connector into a USB slot in your PC.

2. Insert the USB-connector software disc into your PC.

3. Follow the installation instructions.

4. Run the Nintendo Wi-Fi USB Connector Registration Tool.

   Your Wii will appear in the tool window (**Figure 2.21**).

Figure 2.21
When you run the Connector Registration Tool, you see all the Wii units that you can connect to (in this case, Buster).

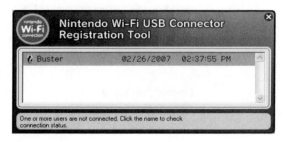

5. Right-click the Wii, and choose Grant Permission to Connect from the shortcut menu (**Figure 2.22**).

Figure 2.22
By right-clicking the Wii you want to connect to (in this case, Buster), you can grant permission to connect.

6. Click the Nintendo Wi-Fi USB Connector option (**Figure 2.23**).

Figure 2.23
When you set up an Internet connection, you get these three choices. When you're connecting through a Nintendo Wi-Fi USB Connector, click that button to complete the job.

7. When the PC is set up, click OK in the Wii screen.

The Wii tests the connection, and voilà—you're connected.

Connecting via LAN cable

When this book was being written (early 2007), the Wii LAN adapter, which will connect to the Wii via one of the two USB ports, was not available from Nintendo. To connect to the Internet with this cable, however, you should be able simply to connect the LAN adapter, plug in the Internet connection, and select Wired Connection in the Internet screen of Wii Settings.

3

The Channels

The Wii Channels are available in the form of miniature television-style screens tiled on the main Wii menu (**Figure 3.1**). These channels are your Wii's

Figure 3.1
The main screen of the Wii.

windows to the world, so to speak, allowing you to access the Internet, all things Mii, photographs, weather forecasts, shopping, and the various Virtual Console games that you've bought and downloaded to your Wii.

The Wii has eight main channels, each of which gives you access to a different aspect of the Wii experience. The Disc Channel, the Mii Channel, and the Photo Channel don't require Internet access, but the Wii Shop Channel, the Forecast Channel, the News Channel, the Everybody Votes Channel, and the Internet Channel are completely dependent on Internet access for their functioning.

This chapter examines the important aspects of the eight main Wii Channels, showing you their functionality and use as they pertain to both experienced and novice Wii users.

Disc Channel

The Disc Channel always appears in the top-left corner of the Wii's main menu; the image it displays correlates to whatever disc is currently inserted into the Wii. When no disc is in the drive, this channel displays a picture of a Wii disc and a GameCube disc, as shown in **Figure 3.2**; it's in ready state, waiting for you to insert a disc.

Figure 3.2
The Disc
Channel waits
for a disc.

Channel Arrows

When you look at the close-up view of any particular channel, you'll notice arrows on either side of the screen (**Figure 3.3**). These arrows, when you select them, cause the channel to slide to the left or right of the current channel. In other words, clicking those arrows is just another way of moving between channels; this way is sequential, taking you through all the available channels one at a time.

Figure 3.3
The arrows on
the sides of the
screen allow
you to navigate
through the
Wii Channels
sequentially.

When you insert a disc into the Wii, the Disc
Channel screen shows either a graphic pertaining
to the software/game (in the case of a Wii game)
or a Nintendo GameCube graphic (in the case of
GameCube games). In **Figure 3.4,** the Wii game
Rayman Raving Rabbids is in the disc drive; therefore,
its graphic is displayed, making it easy for you to see
what game is in the drive and ready to go.

Figure 3.4
When a Wii disc
is in the disc
slot, a graphic
showing the
nature of the
game/software
is displayed
in the Disc
Channel screen.

To swap a disc in the drive and thereby change
what's on the Disc Channel, simply press the Eject
button on the front of the Wii console. The present
disc slides out so you can grab it and put it away. To
insert a different disc, simply place it in the mouth of
the slot, as shown in **Figure 3.5;** the disc gets sucked
into the Wii. Before you know it, the software on the
disc you just inserted is displayed in the Wii Channel
screen as a valid option.

Figure 3.5
Inserting a disc simply requires placing an edge inside the slot; the Wii sucks the disc into place.

Mii Channel

The Mii Channel (**Figure 3.6**) is the place where all things Mii take place. Incidentally, the word *Mii* is pronounced "me," making it great for all you folks who grew up in the 1980s, largely accepted as being the "Me" decade. As comedian Dennis Miller said, the '90s were the "Me me me me me" decade, so maybe the first decade of the new millennium can be the "Mii" decade and avert the nasty subtext.

Figure 3.6
The Mii Channel is the place where your alter ego can go crazy.

Miis are simply miniature versions of you. In the online world, characters such as Miis are called *avatars*, which are graphic representations of how you want people to see you. With Miis, you can create exactly what you want, whether it's an accurate portrait of you or a representation of what you'd like to be. Miis are there for you to mold as you see fit. The Miis that you create or invite to your Mii Plaza (covered later in this chapter) end up as characters in many of the games you play, so having Miis adds a fascinating, endearing, and entertaining wrinkle to the Wii's lovability.

When you create a Mii, you have the option of allowing it to travel. If a Mii travels, it can show up on a stranger's Wii on the other side of the world. Likewise, other people's Miis show up on your Wii from time to time as well. The whole concept is a lot of fun. You can also send Miis directly to a fellow Wii user by mailing them from Mii Plaza.

note   When a Mii travels, it doesn't disappear from your Wii, so don't worry that allowing a Mii to travel means that you'll lose it for a while. You won't.

For a much more in-depth look at Miis, the Mii Channel, and everything else Mii related, check out Chapter 4, which is dedicated to the subject of me ... I mean, Mii.

Hanging with the Miis

Miis tend to congregate in a couple of places, the first of which is Mii Plaza (**Figure 3.7**). This spot is where all the Miis you create on your Wii mingle. They tend to walk around; have conversations; and generally stand ready for those times when you need to use them in a game, in an activity, or in some other software.

Figure 3.7
Mii Plaza is Mii Central for all your Mii-related needs.

Mii Plaza

In Mii Plaza, you can create a Mii; edit an existing Mii; save a Mii to your Wii Remote; email a Mii to another Wii user; or organize your Miis in several ways. In short, Mii Plaza is the hub of Mii activity—the place where you can engage in most Mii activities. Pressing the plus (+) and minus (–) buttons on the Wii Remote allows you to zoom in and out on the Miis in the Plaza, and clicking the whistle icon in the bottom-right corner causes the Miis to come to attention and line up for your inspection.

Mii Parade

The Mii Parade, shown in **Figure 3.8** (on the next page), is where traveling Miis come into your Wii system to hang out. Occasionally, it's a good idea to go to the Mii Parade area to check out whether any

Miis are tooling around there. If so, you can leave them alone; get rid of them; or invite them to your Mii Plaza, where they become part of your Mii community.

Creating and editing Miis

Two buttons in Mii Plaza let you create and edit Miis. When creating a Mii, you can build it completely from scratch or choose a look-alike to help you get the process started. **Figure 3.9** shows an intermediate step in the selection of a look-alike to create a Mii.

Figure 3.9
Choosing a
look-alike in
the process of
creating a Mii.

Editing Miis is highly individual. If you get a new pair of glasses or a new haircut, you may want to edit your Mii to reflect the new you, or you may want to give your Mii the Mohawk you've always wanted. Again, check out Chapter 4 for a detailed breakdown on Mii creation and management.

You cannot edit other people's Mii creations—only those that were created on your Wii system.

Photo Channel

The Photo Channel is a place of great fun and creativity, but you need an SD Memory Card to get your photos into the Wii in the first place. The SD card (**Figure 3.10**) is a small memory device that's nonvolatile but can be written over and erased ad infinitum. SD cards are often the storage medium of choice for owners of digital cameras, so it's easy to get photos into a Wii.

Figure 3.10
A 512 MB SD Memory Card from SanDisk, one of the most popular makers of this sort of card.

For now, I'll assume that you can get your photos onto an SD card, but if you don't understand what I'm talking about, check out Chapter 9 for an explanation of SD cards and a method for getting your digital photographs into your Wii.

At first blush, the Photo Channel (**Figure 3.11**) doesn't seem to have a heck of a lot going for it, but dig just below the surface, and you find that you can have quite a bit of family fun with this channel. Offering everything from slideshows to miniquizzes to the chance to goof with someone's looks in a photo, the Photo Channel is a surprising addition to the Wii universe.

Figure 3.11
The Photo Channel start screen.

Photo views

To add photos to the Wii, you need to insert a photo-laden SD card into the SD card slot on the front of the Wii console (see the diagram in Chapter 2). Many digital cameras and camera cell phones use SD cards as their main form of memory; if this is the case with your photo device, you're all set.

When the SD card is in place in the Wii, click the Start button in the Photo Channel screen to get to the photo-selection screen, shown in **Figure 3.12**.

Figure 3.12
Choose the area from which you want to get your photos.

When the photos are found, the Wii displays first a screen that says Found *X* photos (where *X* is the number) and then a View button. Click the View button to see the photos in question. The photos come up in a nicely displayed grid, as shown in **Figure 3.13**. You have four options at your immediate disposal: Zoom – and Zoom +, which shrink and magnify the current view; Back, which takes you to the preceding screen; and Slide Show, which starts an automatic slideshow of all the pictures available. You can select any photo by clicking it, or you can choose the Slide Show option to start a slideshow.

Figure 3.13
Your photos are displayed in a tasteful grid.

Individual photos

To view an individual photo, click it, and it zooms up to fill the screen (**Figure 3.14**). From this screen, you can rotate the photo; post it to the Wii Message Board; start a slideshow; zoom in or out on the picture; or have some fun with it. To post a photo to the Wii Message Board, you need only click the Post button; to rotate, click the arrow icons in the top-center portion of the screen. (I discuss the Fun! area a little later in the chapter.)

Figure 3.14
Clicking an individual photo brings it up to full-screen size.

Slideshows

To watch a slideshow, click the Slide Show button any time you see it, either in the main photo screen (where your pictures appear as thumbnails) or in the individual-picture screen. When you click the button, the Wii displays a 3-2-1 countdown that looks like the start of an old movie; then it shows your photos one at a time, with music playing in the background.

The other cool thing about slideshows on the Wii is that the photos are subjected to what's commonly called the Ken Burns Effect. (Ken Burns makes great documentaries about subjects including the American Civil War, baseball, and jazz. He pioneered the technique of panning and zooming still photos to create the effect of motion where none existed, because only still images were taken of the Civil War, of course.) The Wii uses this effect beautifully to display your slideshows.

If you press the A button during a slideshow, you get three option buttons (**Figure 3.15**): Resume Slide Show, Change Settings, and Back. If you choose Change Settings, you go to the Slide-Show Settings screen (**Figure 3.16**), where you can alter several aspects of your slideshow. The first thing you can change is the order of pictures; the Wii can display them in file-date order or move through them randomly.

Figure 3.15
By clicking this button, you can alter the settings of the slideshow.

Figure 3.16
The Slide-Show Settings screen.

The second button in the settings screen lets you change the slideshow effects, rotating through three options: Simple, Nostalgic, and Dramatic. The default setting is Dramatic, which provides the motion-laden Ken Burns Effect. The Simple setting displays each picture in a plain, standard slideshow manner, with no fancy motion. The Nostalgic setting, however, gives each photograph a sepia-tone coloration (effectively making all photos look old) while maintaining the dramatic Ken Burns Effect. Ultimately, how the Wii presents your slideshow is up to you.

Another cool option that you can add to your slideshows is music. Click the Choose Song button, and select one of the six instrumental songs that the Wii offers. But fortunately for those of us who like to listen to our own type of music, you can enjoy whatever music you want. In the Choose Song screen is a button that says Other Music. When you click this button, you get instructions for putting your own music into a slideshow (**Figure 3.17**).

Figure 3.17
You can put your own MP3 files on the Wii to play whatever music you like behind slideshows.

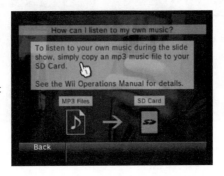

Getting your own songs onto the Wii is simple enough: Just copy MP3 files to your SD card, and they show up in your music list when you set up your slideshows. Check out Chapter 9 for details on how to get MP3 files onto your SD card.

Other photo fun

You can have lots of fun with pictures by clicking the Fun! button (**Figure 3.18**) when you view an individual photo. After you click this button, the Fun! screen appears, featuring three buttons: Mood, Doodle, and Puzzle. All three of these buttons can create plenty of laughs for friends and family.

Figure 3.18
Have some
fun with your
photos!

Mood

The first option in the Fun! screen is Mood. The Mood area (**Figure 3.19**) gives you the option to alter your photos in four distinct ways:

- **Brighten.** This option makes the photo brighter, which can be handy for pictures that are a little too dark to begin with.

- **Black and White.** Not surprisingly, this option strips away all the color information, making your picture pure black and white.

- **Zap!** This option turns your photo into a photographic negative, which can produce some rather interesting results.

- **Hard-Boiled.** This option turns the photo into an image that resembles a picture photocopied from a newspaper article.

Figure 3.19
The Mood area.

Doodle

The second area is Doodle (**Figure 3.20**), where you can write all over your photos in pretty much any color you want. The Wii provides electronic crayons in seven colors, an eraser, and an eyedropper tool that lets you match the color of the writing utensil to any color already in the photo. Doodle also allows you to zoom in and out of the photo for detail work, and it lets you add kisses, hearts, stars, and even sunglasses to provide pizzazz.

Figure 3.20
The Doodle area is popular with my kids.

> **tip**
>
> When you add an object such as sunglasses or a kiss in the Doodle editor, notice that the proximity of the Wii Remote to the sensor bar affects the size of these items. If you want to resize the sunglasses, for example, simply move the remote back a little, and the glasses shrink. Also, you can rotate the items by rotating the Wii Remote.

Puzzle

The last button in the Fun! screen is Puzzle. When you click this button, the current picture becomes a six-piece puzzle that you must solve (**Figure 3.21**). When you finish, the Wii displays the time it took you to complete the puzzle. Even better, however, is that completing the puzzle gives you the option of moving on to a more complex puzzle with 6, 12, 24, or even 48 pieces (**Figure 3.22**). The Puzzle area is surprisingly entertaining, as players race against the clock to put together the puzzle faster than their predecessors did.

Figure 3.21
The six-piece puzzle isn't too tough.

Figure 3.22
When you complete the smaller puzzle, you can ratchet all the way up to 48 pieces.

tip If you're having trouble, clicking the Cheat button zips the picture into its complete shape so that you can get a quick look at how you're supposed to arrange the puzzle pieces.

Wii Shop Channel

A shopping channel on the Wii? Yes, it's true, but it's probably not the kind of shopping channel you have in mind. The Wii Shop Channel (as it's officially called) is a place where you can purchase and download games and other software for the Virtual Console, as well as a place to get nongaming software such as the Everybody Votes Channel and the Opera Web browser for the Internet Channel.

The Wii Shop Channel (**Figure 3.23**) runs on Wii Points, which you can purchase in retail stores as Wii Points Cards; you can also buy them online with a credit card. For a detailed view of the Shop Channel, check out Chapter 7.

Figure 3.23
The front page of the Wii Shop Channel.

Wii Ware

The Wii Ware area is the part of the Shop Channel that offers nongaming applications for the Wii. These applications are often free and are sometimes in incomplete beta form, but that doesn't mean that they aren't functional and useful.

At this writing, the Everybody Votes Channel is available for download through the Wii Ware area, as is
the Opera Web browser (which is currently free but
eventually will cost 500 to 1,000 Wii Points). This
channel is free to all users and is supposed to remain
that way. In fact, by the time you purchase your Wii
(if you haven't already), the Everybody Votes Channel
may very well be included, eliminating the need to
download or update it.

Virtual Console

The Virtual Console area is where you can purchase
games for the Wii's Virtual Console—a feature that
takes advantage of the Wii's power and flexibility
by enabling it to play games made for long-since-
dead gaming systems. The Virtual Console includes
games for the Nintendo Entertainment System,
Super Nintendo, Nintendo 64, Sega Genesis, and
TurboGrafx 16 (**Figure 3.24**). Many of the games offered
here are absolute classics that even youngsters jaded
by today's technology can still find enjoyable.

Figure 3.24
The Virtual
Console area
sells games for
five old gaming
systems.

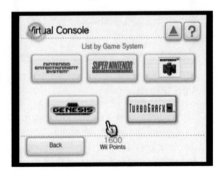

Check out Chapter 7 for more details on the Virtual Console area in the Shop Channel, and see Chapter 8 to learn about the Virtual Console in general.

Forecast Channel

The Forecast Channel is a great spot that lets you download weather reports and long-term forecasts into your Wii (via the WiiConnect24 service). When you start the Forecast Channel, the Wii helps you select the city or town nearest your location, the temperature display (degrees Fahrenheit or Celsius), and the way wind speed is represented. Then the forecast for your location comes up on the screen, as shown in **Figure 3.25**.

Figure 3.25
The Forecast Channel is a treat to watch.

note The WiiConnect24 service is Nintendo's way of ensuring that the Wii is connected to the Internet all the time, so that traveling Miis, mail, weather reports, and news can come to the device around the clock, putting current information at your fingertips whenever you sit in front of the Wii. Check out Chapter 6 for more detail on the WiiConnect24 service.

In the main Forecast Channel screen, you see the current temperature and conditions; at the click of a button, you can also see the UV index, change the settings, or look at the forecasted temperatures for today or this week.

Perhaps the best feature of the Forecast Channel is the Globe (**Figure 3.26**), which allows you to check out temperatures around the world simply by putting a Wii Remote "hand" on the globe and spinning the globe to the locations you want to see.

Figure 3.26
The Globe feature (the images come from NASA) is spectacular.

tip

If you zoom out far enough in the Globe feature, you can see the stars around the Earth. These stars are apparently accurate; not being an astronomer, I'm unable to confirm that.

News Channel

The News Channel is very much like the Forecast Channel except that it contains information about news rather than weather. What news the Wii displays is skewed toward the location where you live, but you still have access to news from the world over.

When you access the News Channel, expect a short delay while the news items are downloaded. Then you get a main page that displays several news headings: National News, International News, Sports, Arts/Entertainment, Business, Science/Health, and Technology.

Viewing news items

As you move through and select the main headings in the News Channel, individual news stories appear, with the first few words of each story displayed. Sometimes, the Wii displays a small picture as well (**Figure 3.27**). Clicking a news item brings up the article in readable form, along with any available

Figure 3.27 Stories are listed in this fashion, with the occasional picture present.

pictures. To modify the scale of the picture and the size of the text, press the + (plus) and – (minus) buttons on the Wii Remote.

Highlighting text

If you are reading a particular story and want to point out some text to someone else in the room, you can highlight that text. Press the 1 button while moving over the text to bring up a red pencil, which highlights the text you're moving over (**Figure 3.28**).

Figure 3.28
The red pencil can come in handy when you want to point out text to someone.

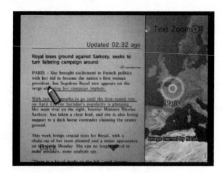

The News Globe

When you're viewing an International News item, the specific
area where the story is set appears on the right side of the screen.
If you click this map, you get a large globe view that's not unlike
the Forecast Channel's Globe feature. In this view, you can see
news items from all over the world, and if you tilt the viewpoint
by clicking the arrow keys on the screen, you can determine the
number of news items about specific locations by the height of
their stacks (**Figure 3.29**).

Figure 3.29
The globe view
in the News
Channel shows
news stories in
stacks.

Everybody Votes Channel

This channel launched in February 2007 and is available from the Wii Ware area of the Wii Shop Channel. The Everybody Votes Channel (**Figure 3.30**) is a unique idea, in that it allows up to six users of a single Wii to vote on a series of questions that are tallied both locally and worldwide.

Figure 3.30
Everybody Votes is an entertaining channel, if a little tame.

The first thing you have to do is register some Miis to vote—as many as six per household. To register a Mii, select it in the Mii list. Then select the question you want to vote on. Questions are listed on the main page. You can also click the Worldwide Polls button to find other questions to vote on.

After you select the question you want to vote on, you go to a large circular area where you pick up your Mii and move it to one answer or the other. (Answers are color coded.) This action casts your vote.

Next, you are asked whether you want to predict the vote's outcome. Predicting the vote's outcome is different from voting, in that you are trying to guess how most people will vote rather than giving your opinion. When you're done, that's it; you need to wait until the vote's time limit is up (usually, several days). To view the results of a vote, select the results that you want to see; hordes of miniature Miis stream in to show you graphically what the results are. **Figure 3.31** shows an example of voting results.

Figure 3.31
Looks like more people want to live at the beach.

The Everybody Votes Channel is engaging, but the questions tend to be on the inane side and are generally more for children than for adults. Still, it's interesting to watch the technology in action, and it's fun to sit down with your kids and see how each vote transpired.

Internet Channel

The software for the Internet Channel (**Figure 3.32**) is available by download from the Wii Shop Channel. At this writing, the software is free, but Nintendo plans to charge for it eventually. The software in question is the Opera browser, which works pretty much like any other Web browser. Indeed, you can use the Internet Channel to visit an unlimited number of Web sites, so be aware when your kids are using it.

Figure 3.32
The Internet
Channel is a
Web browser.

The browser offers three areas: Favorites, Enter a Web Address, and Help. The Favorites area (**Figure 3.33**) is like a bookmarks area in Microsoft's Internet Explorer or Apple's Safari browser, which is to say that when you go to a site you want the program to remember, you can mark it as a favorite.

Figure 3.33
Mark your favorites as you come by them.

To enter a Web address, click the WWW button in the main Internet Channel screen; then use your cursor to enter the address just as you would in a normal Web browser (**Figure 3.34**), and click the OK button to go to that Web site.

Figure 3.34
Entering a Web site's address is a breeze, if a little slow—one character at a time.

Currently, the Internet Channel is just for Web browsing, but the browser is as powerful as most similar browsers, and you can do almost everything with it that you could on a PC. Check out Chapter 6 to learn a little more about the Internet Channel.

4

Mii and You

Part of what makes the world of the Wii so special is the existence of Miis (*Mii* is pronounced "me"), which are little cartoon characters that represent you in the Wii universe. Miis can be anything you want them to be, so you can design them to look as much—or as little—like you as your heart desires. If you want, you can make a different Mii for every day of the week, or if you're feeling really avant-garde, you can create a Mii that represents both the male and female aspects of your personality.

In other words, when it comes to creating Miis, the sky is the limit. This chapter is here to show you how to squeeze every last drop of creativity out of Miis in the Wii universe.

note Everything that happens directly with Miis, with the exception of attaching Miis to emails that you send out of the main Wii screen, happens in the Mii Channel. Therefore, whatever I discuss in this chapter relates to the Mii Channel unless I note otherwise.

Why Mii?

If you haven't spent a fair bit of time with a Wii, no doubt you wonder why Miis populate the Wii in the first place. That's a good question. But when you start playing some games on the Wii, toying with software, and communicating with your friends and acquaintances via Wii Mail, you soon realize why Miis play a special role in making the Wii such an engaging machine.

Miis are recordkeepers for many games and activities that you play and enjoy on the Wii. When you play Wii Sports games, for example, the onscreen characters are pulled directly from Mii Plaza (**Figure 4.1**). In Wii Sports Baseball, for example, characters from Mii

Figure 4.1
Contestants in Wii Sports Boxing come straight from Mii Plaza.

Plaza are used as fielders and batters. This feature adds an air of familiarity to many of the games you play on the Wii, making extra fun for individual players when their Miis are the focus of attention.

Miis are an important part of allowing you to identify with the onscreen actions of the Wii; they give you a sense of ownership that other consoles just don't provide. When you vote in the Everybody Votes Channel, you vote with your personally created Mii (**Figure 4.2**). This sort of connection with the games and activities makes Miis an integral part of the Wii's success.

Figure 4.2
In the Everybody Votes Channel, Miis are used as the voters.

Making a Mii

So now that you know what a Mii is, you need to dive straight in and make yourself a Mii so that you can be represented in the Wii universe. To make a Mii, go into the Mii Channel; then click the Start button, which takes you to Mii Plaza. Click the New Mii button on the left side of the screen. You go to a screen that allows you to choose between a male and a female Mii.

The following sections discuss the various aspects of creating a Mii.

Where to start

When it comes to creating a Mii, you can take two basic paths. One path involves choosing a prefab-ricated face for your Mii, and the other involves building the Mii's face from scratch. As soon as you select the gender of your Mii, you can start from scratch or choose your Mii's face from a page of look-alikes.

If you start from scratch, you'll literally build your Mii from the ground up. If you don't want to spend the time tinkering with minutia, go the look-alike route, which gives you multitudes of faces to choose among (**Figure 4.3**).

Figure 4.3
The choices of look-alike Miis are extensive.

No matter which choice you make, you end up in the Mii Editor, and you have access to all the tools available for altering the Mii. The following section looks at the nine distinct tools available for altering your Mii.

Building your Mii

Whether you start building your Mii from a prefabricated model or create it from scratch, the process of altering or creating a Mii is similar.

If you choose to go the look-alike route, you start with a face that's already in place, and you can alter it or choose not to. But if you choose to build your own Mii, you need to move through each tool to build your Mii.

To modify or build a Mii from scratch, follow these steps:

1. Go to the Mii Channel, and click the Start button.

   You arrive in Mii Plaza.

2. Click the New Mii button on the left side of the screen (**Figure 4.4**).

Figure 4.4
Start by clicking New Mii.

3. Choose your Mii's gender (**Figure 4.5**); then click Start from Scratch.

Figure 4.5
A big question: Is your Mii male or female?

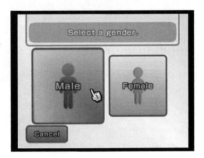

4. Click the first button in the row of buttons at the top of the screen; then enter a name for your Mii, give it a birthday (which could be your own), choose the Mii's favorite color, and identify the Mii's creator (**Figure 4.6**).

Figure 4.6
Choose the first set of options for your Mii in this screen.

If you also want to give your Mii a nickname, click the Nickname box; the Wii displays a virtual keyboard (**Figure 4.7**) that you can use to enter the nickname.

Figure 4.7
Enter the Mii's
nickname in
this screen.

If you choose here to make your Mii one of your
Favorites, you can organize it that way in Mii
Plaza later.

Deciding whether your new Mii mingles
(**Figure 4.8**) is important, because a Mii that
mingles will travel to other consoles and join
other people's Mii Parades. (I guess you could
look at this option as being a nonbiological way
of reproducing.) See the "Traveling Miis" sidebar
in this section for more details. To set your Mii to
mingle, click the Mingle box (refer to Figure 4.6).

Figure 4.8
Your Mii can
be a world
traveler—or not.

5. Click the second button over at the top of the screen to set the height and weight of your Mii (**Figure 4.9**).

Figure 4.9
Losing weight and gaining height have never been easier.

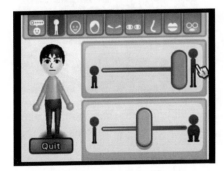

6. Click the third button over at the top of the screen to go to the head area, where you can use the top row of buttons to choose the basic shape of your Mii's head and its skin color (**Figure 4.10**).

You have six choices of skin color—enough to allow you to express a reasonable amount of racial diversity.

Figure 4.10
Pick a head shape and skin color.

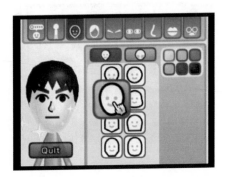

The 12-button grid below the basic head-shape buttons (**Figure 4.11**) lets you add facial features—age lines, bags under or around the eyes, rosy cheeks, and even eye shadow—to tweak the Mii's looks even further.

Figure 4.11
Customize your Mii's face here.

7. Click the fourth button over at the top of the screen to do your Mii's hair (**Figure 4.12**).

You have 72 distinct hairstyles to choose among, roughly divided into male and female areas, as well as 8 hair colors.

Figure 4.12
For each of the 72 hairstyles, you can swap the part from right to left, or vice versa.

tip Many hairstyles are unisexual and can be used successfully by either gender. When I created the Beatles for my Mii Plaza, for example, I had to use two female hair styles (for John Lennon and George Harrison) to successfully approximate their looks.

8. Click the fifth button to set the eyebrows (**Figure 4.13**), which come in 24 flavors, including no eyebrows at all.

   Choose any of eight colors for these amusing strips of hair. You can also move the eyebrows up or down and left or right, tilt them, and move them closer together or farther apart. You can even change their size dramatically. (Mr. Spock, here I come!)

Figure 4.13
Express your
Mii's personality
through
eyebrows.

9. Click the sixth button to adjust the eye shape (**Figure 4.14**).

   You can alter each of the 48 eye styles the same way that you adjust the eyebrows: closer together or farther apart, up or down on the face, tilted up or down, and smaller or larger. You also have a choice of six eye colors, from evil black to groovy green.

Figure 4.14
Eye color can have a dramatic effect when you choose certain eye shapes.

> **tip**
>
> I highly recommend that when you choose the particulars for your Mii's eyes, you take your time and try out a multitude of options. The eyes, as some say, are the windows to the soul, and the eye options give you so much flexibility that it's worth taking the time to get your Mii's eyes just right.

10. Click the seventh button to fix your Mii's nose (**Figure 4.15**).

You have 12 basic options to choose among. The important modifiers are the size and placement controls, which allow you to move the nose up and down on the face and change its size dramatically.

Figure 4.15
The size and shape of the nose can make an amazing difference in a Mii's appearance.

11. Click the eighth button to set the mouth (**Figure 4.16**).

Figure 4.16
You have plenty of eclectic mouth choices for your Mii.

The mouth screen has 24 options, some of which are a little more on the feminine or masculine side than others, but all of them are acceptable for any Mii. If you're using full lips, you can choose among three lip tones, ranging from flesh color to pink. As with the eyebrows, nose, and eyes, you can alter the position (up or down on the face) and size of the lips.

12. Click the ninth button to add accessories (**Figure 4.17**).

Your options include facial hair, eyeglasses, and beauty marks. When you choose a particular accessory (such as eyeglasses), you get options for tweaking that accessory.

Figure 4.17
If you want shades on your Mii, you can have them.

13. When you're satisfied with your Mii, click the Quit button; then click the Save and Quit button to save your Mii and end the process.

   You return to Mii Plaza, where your new Mii drops into place (**Figure 4.18**).

Figure 4.18
This Mii is not to be confused with any actual person, living or dead.

note If you are working on your Wii and want to edit a Mii that you didn't create, unfortunately, you're out of luck. Still, if you are just dying to do it, you *can* edit that Mii on your PC or on the Web by using one of the third-party Mii editing tools. (See "Editing Miis Outside the Wii" later in this chapter.) This ability is one of the key reasons for a person to use a third-party Mii editor.

Traveling Miis

When you create a Mii, you have the option to let the Mii mingle. When you set the Mingle option, your Mii (actually, a copy of it) moves about the Internet and jumps into other people's Wii units so that they can use your Mii for their own purposes. Likewise, other people's Miis find their way to the Mii Parade on your Wii.

If you want other people's Miis to travel to your Wii, it's best to have WiiConnect24 activated (see Chapter 6). That way, your Wii is always ready to receive Miis from other Wii consoles.

To see whether any visitors have shown up on your Wii, go to the Mii Parade area. If you find some guest Miis doing the parade thing, you can pick them up and drop them in your Mii Plaza, effectively adding them to your Wii for future use. If you don't like the look of any new Miis in your Mii Parade area, simply drag them to the Erase button.

Navigating Mii Plaza

Mii Plaza is the place where Miis hang around, ready for you to inspect or alter them. The Plaza has nine basic command buttons on the left and right sides of the screen (**Figure 4.19**).

Wii Menu

Edit Mii

Create Mii

Erase Mii

Help

Mii Parade

Transfer Mii

Wii Friend

Arrange

Figure 4.19
Mii's Plaza's command buttons.

In counterclockwise order from the top-left corner of the screen, the buttons are:

- **Wii Menu.** This button returns you to the main Wii screen.

- **Edit Mii.** This button allows you to edit any aspect of a Mii.

note You can edit only Miis that were created on your Wii, so Miis that came from other users over the Internet are off limits for modification. (Bummer.)

- **Create Mii.** This button takes you to the area where you can create a Mii from a facial template or create it from scratch (refer to "Making a Mii" earlier in this chapter).

- **Erase Mii.** As the name implies, dropping a Mii onto this button erases the Mii. Not to worry if you drop the Mii on this button accidentally; you must click a button in a dialog box to confirm your intention to delete the Mii.

- **Help.** Clicking the Help button gives you what it says: help.

- **Arrange.** This button enables you to arrange the Miis in Mii Plaza by various criteria, including gender, name, and size (see "Arranging Miis" later in this chapter).

- **Wii Friend.** This button allows you to email your Miis to another Wii user. The only caveat is that you need to know the other Wii owner's Wii Number (see the sidebar "The Wii Address Book" later in this chapter).

- **Transfer Mii.** Click this button to place as many as ten Miis on your Wii Remote and ultimately transport them to another Wii system.

- **Mii Parade.** This button takes you to the Mii Parade area, where Miis that have come to your Wii via the Internet parade up and down the screen endlessly.

Managing Miis

When your Miis are populating your Mii Plaza, you have a few ways to manage them, keep track of them, and generally manipulate them. The basic way to identify an individual Mii is to move your cursor over the Mii and then press the A button on your Wii Remote; a bubble pops up that shows the Mii's name, and the Mii turns toward you so that you can see its face (**Figure 4.20**).

Figure 4.20
Clicking a Mii causes it to face you and display its name.

The following sections discuss the various commands and techniques for managing Miis in Mii Plaza.

Zooming

Mii Plaza tends to be set at a particular magnification, allowing you to see just enough detail of the Miis to pick them out. If you click a Mii with the A button on your remote, the Mii's name appears above it, but to get a closer look at a Mii or a group of Miis, you need to press the plus (+) key on the

Wii Remote to zoom in on the action, as shown in **Figure 4.21**. Not surprisingly, if you zoom in with the + key, you can zoom back out with the minus (–) key just as easily. These controls are duplicated onscreen, but it's easier to use the remote.

Figure 4.21
A group of Miis in close-up mode after you zoom in with the Wii Remote.

Grabbing Miis

If you want to pick up a Mii in Mii Plaza, put your cursor over the Mii and simultaneously press the A and B buttons on the Wii Remote. The Mii gets picked up by its head, and its arms and legs flail dramatically (**Figure 4.22**). Even the Wii Remote gives you physical feedback that you are holding a squirming entity! When you have the Mii in your grasp, you can move it to the Wii Friend, Edit Mii, or Erase Mii button.

Figure 4.22
You can pick up a Mii by simultaneously pressing the A and B buttons on the Wii Remote.

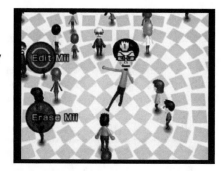

Arranging Miis

If you click the Arrange button—the whistle icon—all the Miis immediately move into a grid, standing at attention so that you can inspect them (**Figure 4.23**). When the Miis are in this grid, you can arrange them alphabetically, by their status as favorites, by the color of their clothing, and by gender.

Figure 4.23
Miis being arranged.

Sending a Mii to a friend

If you want to send a Mii to a friend, you need only click the Wii Friend button (the envelope icon). Then pick up the Mii you want to send (refer to "Grabbing Miis" earlier in this chapter), and drag it to the envelope icon at the top-center of the screen, as shown in **Figure 4.24**.

Figure 4.24
Drag the Mii you want to send.

After you've moved the Mii to the envelope icon, you get a list of Wii owners to whom you can send the Mii (**Figure 4.25**). Click the appropriate name, and you're done. You return to Mii Plaza, where the Mii you just sent lands unceremoniously in the middle of the Plaza, and you get a message saying that the Mii was sent to the person you chose. The process is easy, requiring only that you already have your Wii Friends listed in your address book (see the sidebar "The Wii Address Book").

Figure 4.25
Click a button
to pick the lucky
recipient of your
Mii.

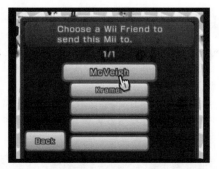

The Wii Address Book

Although emailing is covered in detail in Chapter 6, it's worth mentioning the Wii Address Book here to show you how to figure out your Wii's number and how to get names into the address book.

I suspect that Wii newbies may have trouble finding their Wii's 16-digit Wii Number. Most people start looking in the Settings area, but you actually find the Wii Number by clicking the Wii Message Board icon in the bottom-right corner of the Wii's main screen and then clicking the Create Message button, as shown in **Figure 4.26**.

Figure 4.26
To get to the
Wii Number,
you first have
to get to the
address book
through the
Create Message
button.

(continues on next page)

The Wii Address Book (continued)

When you're in the Create Message area, simply click the Address Book icon, shown in **Figure 4.27**, and you see the Wii Number for your device. The Wii Number always appears on the front page of your address book so that you can get to it quickly and easily. I recommend, however, that you write this number down, because it's common for people to ask you for this number via email (on your computer) or through other non-Wii means.

Figure 4.27
A unit's Wii Number is displayed on the front of the Wii Address Book.

To enter a new name into your address book, you need that person's Wii Number. After you've done that, you can send messages and Miis to fellow Wii users with ease.

Transferring Miis

One of the great features of the Wii Remote is that it can hold as many as ten Miis in storage. These Miis can be transferred to other Wii units or held on the Wii Remote indefinitely.

note   When a Mii is transferred to a Wii Remote, it isn't removed from the Wii unit. A Mii that resides on the Wii Remote is just a copy of the Mii that resides on the Wii console.

To transfer one or more Miis to your Wii Remote, click the Transfer Mii button; when the screen showing the connected Wii Remotes appears, click the Wii Remote that you want to transfer the Miis to. **Figure 4.28** shows this process for a Wii that has only one Wii Remote connected.

Figure 4.28
Choose the remote where you want to transfer the Miis.

The Wii Remote's Save panel opens, showing ten circles, each of which can hold and save one Mii. To save any particular Mii, place your cursor over the Mii; then pick the Mii up (by pressing the A and B buttons on the remote together) and drag it to the save spot, as shown in **Figure 4.29**. When Miis are saved on the Wii Remote, they stay there until you delete them.

Figure 4.29
You can save ten Mii characters on a Wii Remote.

To put saved Miis on someone else's Wii, you simply reverse the process. After the Wii Remote is connected to the machine, click the Transfer Mii button to get the Wii Remote's Save panel to appear; then drag the Miis from the Save panel to the foreign Wii's Mii Plaza.

Editing Miis Outside the Wii

Although the Wii's tools for managing Miis are handy, it's not surprising that several Mii editors have cropped up, both for the PC and for the Web. Why would you want to edit your Mii on the Web or on a home computer? The answer lies in the fact that these editors usually offer features that are not available on the Wii itself, but more important, these editors allow you to edit Miis that you *didn't* create yourself. This capability is a powerful one, because the Wii prevents you from touching any Mii that you didn't personally create.

Because getting your Miis off the Wii and onto your PC can be a difficult, cumbersome process that may require extra equipment, that method of editing Miis is discussed in Chapter 10. That said, the actual Mii-editing software is easy to use and readily available for both Web-based players and Windows software. In this section, I discuss both types of software.

Web-based editors

Several Web-based editors are available as I write this book; it's probably safe to assume that many more are in the works. By the time you read this chapter, a dozen new programs may be available, but most of them will probably work in similar ways.

The two most popular editors are Mii Editor and Wii-volution. Both of these editors are functional and fun to play around with.

Mii Editor

Mii Editor (www.miieditor.com), shown in **Figure 4.30**, is a full online editor. Still in beta form, it looks and functions exactly like the Mii Editor on the Wii. The only difference is that the online editor lets you import and export Mii files.

Figure 4.30
The Web-based Mii Editor in action.

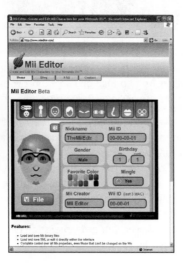

note Mii Editor requires Adobe's Flash Player 9.0.28.0 or later. The download for the Flash player is entirely free and available from Adobe's Web site (www.adobe.com).

To save or load Mii files, click the File button to go to the Files screen (**Figure 4.31**). Here, you can save and load your creations for later transfer to a Wii Remote and ultimately to a foreign Wii.

Figure 4.31
The Files screen in Mii Editor.

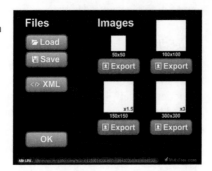

Mii Editor gives you control of all Mii properties, and you can load and save all Mii binary files for modification. As a bonus, you can export your Mii to a JPEG file for use as an avatar somewhere else.

Figure 4.32
The Randomize feature is interesting, to say the least.

One key difference between the Wii's built-in editor and the Web-based Mii Editor is the Randomize feature, which you access via a small die in the top-right corner of the Mii display window. If you click that die, a random set of facial features appears for the Mii under construction. **Figure 4.32** shows just how bizarre a random Mii generation can be. That said, however, random generation can create interesting Miis.

Wii-volution

The Wii-volution editor (**Figure 4.33**) is available at www.wii-volution.com/create-a-mii.html. It differs from the Web-based Mii Editor in that it's a close copy of what's available on the Wii. In other words, you can't create Miis in this editor and then move them to your Wii, and you can't do anything in this editor that you can't do in the Wii Editor. Wii-volution is simply a copycat editor that lets people experiment with the editing tools on the Wii.

Figure 4.33
Wii-volution is a straight-up copy of the built-in Mii Editor on the Wii.

The only real exception is that the graphics in this editor are unique and more 3D than the Wii's built-in graphics. Still, Wii-volution is a fun little editor you can use to experiment when you're bored at work and don't have your Wii handy.

PC-based editors

Two popular PC-based editors are available at this writing. (Sorry, Macintosh fans; nothing's available for the Mac yet.) Wii - M!! Editor and AJ's Mii Editor are nongraphical, dialog-box-based programs, which means that you don't get to see your Mii being built—just the numerical parameters of the various shapes and colors. Still, these editors have some real power; if you're serious about editing Miis, you probably should gravitate to these programs.

 The actual process for transferring Miis to and from a PC is discussed in detail in Chapter 10.

Wii - M!! Editor

Currently up to version 1.2.1, Wii - M!! Editor (**Figure 4.34**) is the most powerful Mii editor available. The software (created by Jamie Magers in Visual Basic) breaks every aspect of a Mii's appearance into exact numeric values, enabling you to adjust the details of a Mii as finely as possible. You can adjust everything about the eyebrows, for example, from type, size, and color to rotation to vertical and horizontal positions. Wii - M!! Editor is a great piece of software for those who love minute detail.

Figure 4.34
Wii - M!! Editor
allows you to
manage your
Miis down to
the last digit.

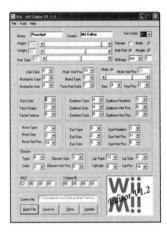

AJ's Mii Editor

AJ's Mii Editor (**Figure 4.35**) is another dialog-box-based editor that displays no graphics but allows you to alter a Mii in extreme ways. The software takes the physical features of your Mii to the far extremes of what's possible, letting you create some very interesting Miis. The one caveat is that you must have Microsoft .NET 2.0 Framework installed on your computer before you can run the software.

Figure 4.35
AJ's Mii Editor
is a great editor,
but you must
have Microsoft
.NET 2.0
Framework to
make it work on
your PC.

AJ's Mii Editor was created by someone who prefers to be known only as AJ187. Despite his or her anonymity, the creator updates the software regularly with bug fixes and minor new features.

 If you don't like to install all sorts of extra background programming languages and frameworks, you may want to use Wii - M!! Editor, because it works straight out of the box (so to speak). AJ's Mii Editor, although it's more flexible, is a little trickier to run.

5

Wii Controllers

I discuss the Wii controllers in reasonable detail in Chapter 1, but because the control system is such an important aspect of the Wii experience and gaming on the Wii, I feel that these devices deserve their very own chapter.

It's not a leap to argue that the Wii Remote and its accessories are what make the Wii a hot-selling item. Indeed, any particular game—and even the Wii's main interface—wouldn't be too impressive if not for the paradigm-shifting controllers.

This chapter looks in detail at the technologies that go into making such a successful wireless environment and also examines the best ways to maximize your control abilities.

The Wii Remote

The backbone of the Wii's control system is the Wii Remote (**Figure 5.1**), a deceptively simple-looking remote control that takes cues from multiple built-in devices so that it can place you in the game/software/realm in 3D.

Figure 5.1
The Wii Remote is a thing of beauty.

The remote can simulate real-life objects as different as a janitor's broom, a baseball bat, an elephant's trunk, and a waiter's service tray. If you think those are just random examples that I pulled out of thin air, prepare to be surprised: Every one of them comes from a game I own.

What makes the Wii Remote tick?

The Wii Remote (sometimes called a *Wiimote* and pronounced "we-mote") is a very cool object that allows users to connect to and interact with the Wii in new ways. But what went into this little device that makes it so darned special? In the following sections, I look inside a Wii Remote to show you what its guts are and what they can do.

Accelerometers

Accelerometer is a fancy-pants name for a little device that measures acceleration. Why would anyone want to measure acceleration? Actually, accelerometers have plenty of useful applications, such as in car airbag systems (sudden deceleration triggers the release of the airbag). Also, some laptop computers have a built-in accelerometer that senses when the computer is dropped (because it's accelerating due to gravity as it falls) and instantly parks the hard drive's head to prevent the disk from being damaged when the computer hits the ground.

Accelerometers sense not only acceleration but also vibration, speed, and inclination. As it turns out, all these capabilities come in *very* handy in creating a wireless remote control for a videogame system.

The Wii Remote contains more than one accelerometer, making it capable of sensing acceleration and movement on multiple axes. The Nunchuk also contains an accelerometer.

Force feedback

Force feedback (also called *rumble*) refers to the Wii Remote's ability to shudder, jolt, rumble, and vibrate during game play. The built-in rumble device makes the remote move in the user's hand, creating a much more realistic gaming experience. Even more important, the physical feedback gives the user valuable cues that help him play the game.

With the Wii Remote, the use of force feedback is so ubiquitous that the device even twitches when the cursor moves over a button you can click. It's hard to describe how useful this feature is until you've had a chance to try it for yourself, but suffice it to say that the combination of visual, audio, and physical feedback makes the Wii Remote even more useful.

Sound

Although some people have maligned the built-in speaker on the Wii Remote, this feature actually adds considerably to both the remote's functionality and the gaming experience as a whole. Some games use the speaker as a gaming device, requiring you to hold the remote up to your ear to listen to instructions during the game.

How does the Wii Remote communicate?

Now you know what's inside the Wii Remote, but you may still wonder how on earth it gets all that information out to the Wii (and how information goes from the Wii to the remote, for that matter). The answer lies in two separate technologies: Bluetooth and infrared.

note For information on how to synchronize a Wii Remote with the Wii, check out Chapter 2.

Bluetooth

To make a long story short, Bluetooth is a communications specification for wireless connections between cell phones and wireless headsets; home computers and wireless mice or keyboards; and a host of other devices, such as printers and digital cameras.

Bluetooth technology turns out to be an ideal communication platform for the Wii Remote, allowing it to communicate with the Wii very quickly. Several times per second, each accelerometer in the Wii Remote sends information to the Wii, and Bluetooth is capable of handling this information flow with ease. The result is smooth, seamless communication between the controller and the console—absolutely essential for creating the feeling of total power that's necessary for a wireless controller.

Bluetooth uses a frequency range in and around the 2.4 GHz realm, which is similar to that of many home cordless telephones, and the maximum effective range of Bluetooth in the Wii is actually around about 30 feet.

 note **Bluetooth communication is only part of how the Wii Remote works, so 30 feet is not the remote's effective range—merely the maximum range at which the information transmitted via Bluetooth can travel.**

Infrared sensing

The Wii Remote has a 1-megapixel image sensor that "sees" the ten infrared LEDs on the sensor bar (**Figure 5.2**) and communicates that information via Bluetooth to the Wii, telling the Wii where the Wii Remote is in space and providing information about its movement. The connected sensor bar uses these infrared lights as another way for the remote to tell where it is in space.

Figure 5.2
The sensor bar is 50 percent of the answer to the communication question.

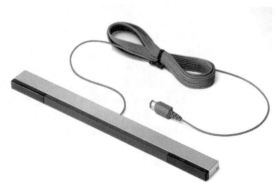

Although you can place the sensor bar above or below your television set, you need to be place it somewhere in line with the center of the TV. Also, it's important to make sure that nothing is blocking the sensor bar. The Wii Remote's interpretation of the size and spacing of the sensor bar's infrared LEDs gives it a great deal of information, including how close the remote is to the sensor bar. For the sensor bar to work properly with your Wii Remote, you need to keep the remote within about 12 feet of the sensor bar (and in visual range of it). The manual says that the sensor bar/remote range is 16 feet, but my nonscientific tests put it at about 12 feet.

Because the range of the remotes for any Wii system is bound to vary among locations (for reasons such as battery strength or electromagnetic interference), you may want to test the range of your remote yourself. Start by getting the Wii Remote's cursor onscreen; then back away from the TV until the cursor disappears. When the cursor disappears, you've reached the point at which the remote no longer communicates with the sensor bar.

note Some users have noted that certain halogen lights or devices that use infrared technology can interfere with the functioning of the Wii Remote. This interference isn't particularly surprising; it stands to reason that any device that uses similar technology may cause some problems with the Wii's sensor bar and remote. If you run into this sort of problems, your only two choices are to move the Wii to another room or to move the offending device from the Wii's area.

Settings

If you want to alter the speaker volume, the presence or absence of rumble, or the connection number (1 to 4) of your Wii Remote, press the Home button in the middle of the remote to get to the screen shown in **Figure 5.3**. In this screen, you can change the volume of the speaker, turn the rumble function on or off, and reconnect remotes to your heart's content.

Figure 5.3
Pressing the Wii Remote's Home button at any time displays this screen, where you can change the speaker volume, turn rumble on or off, and reconnect Wii Remotes.

Calibration

If you are having trouble with your Wii Remote, such as a flickering onscreen cursor (hand) or unexpected onscreen behavior—in other words, if what you do with your remote isn't reflected on your TV—you may need to calibrate the remote.

Calibrating the Wii Remote is relatively easy, and you can do it in less than a minute. Follow these steps:

1. Go to the Wii System Settings 2 screen (main screen > Wii Options > Wii Settings > Wii System Settings 2), and click the Sensor Bar button, shown in **Figure 5.4**.

Figure 5.4
Click the Sensor Bar button.

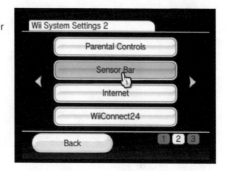

2. Click the Sensitivity button in the next screen (**Figure 5.5**).

   You move to a screen that describes the calibration process.

Figure 5.5
Click the Sensitivity button.

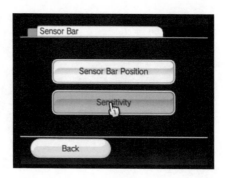

3. Click OK to continue.

The dialog box shown in **Figure 5.6** explains that you need to press the plus (+) and minus (−) buttons on the remote until you see only two dots onscreen.

Figure 5.6
This dialog box explains the calibration process.

4. Click OK in the dialog box.

You move to the calibration screen, which displays two or three dots that are tied to your Wii Remote (**Figure 5.7**); when you move the remote, the dots onscreen move with it.

Figure 5.7
You see two or three dots in the calibration screen.

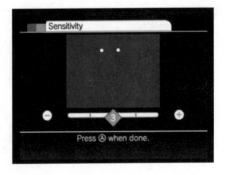

note If you see two blinking dots right off the bat, you don't have to touch anything; press the A button to end the calibration.

5. Move the Wii Remote around gently so that the dots move gently onscreen; then press the + and − buttons as needed until you see only two blinking dots onscreen.

6. Press the A button on the remote to end the calibration.

6

Beyond Gaming

The Wii comes from a company known specifically for games (Nintendo), so what could be "beyond gaming" on a system such as the Wii? As it turns out, the Wii can do a fair bit that's outside the realm of gaming, and with the inclusion of the Forecast Channel, the News Channel, the Photo Channel, and the Everybody Votes Channel, the Wii has immediate and obvious nongaming uses.

Even with the excellent channels that come with the Wii (or that you can download quickly), quite a few other aspects of the Wii make it a useful electronic appliance. Heck, the Wii has even started to become a weight-loss device—and that in itself is worth weighing in on.

The Wii As Internet Appliance

Nintendo has gone out of its way to ensure that the Wii is capable of being *the* Internet appliance for a household. The Wii has many uses that are not game related, from checking weather and news to exchanging mail with friends and enemies. I'm going to look at these uses in this section, so hang on to your hat.

Getting connected

The key to this "Internet appliance" theory of mine is, of course, having a reliable Internet connection. I outline getting connected in detail in Chapter 2, so I won't cover it again here. That said, you must have a connection to the Net, and a high-speed connection is most desirable.

At this writing, you have three ways to connect via high-speed Internet: wireless connection, wireless connection with a Nintendo Wi-Fi USB Connector (**Figure 6.1**), and direct Ethernet connectivity via a

Figure 6.1
The Nintendo Wi-Fi USB Connector is a small device that plugs straight into a computer's USB port.

USB LAN connector. Unfortunately, the USB LAN connector is not available yet, but I assume that it will be available in the coming months.

Staying online with WiiConnect24

Simply put, the WiiConnect24 feature allows the Wii console to communicate with the Internet even when the Wii's power is turned off. As a result, the Wii can receive system updates and traveling Mii characters at any time; it can also run, in the background, games that require connection to the Internet (such as Animal Crossing).

The other major bonus of WiiConnect24 comes to light in the Forecast, Everybody Votes, and News channels. When WiiConnect24 is up and running, the Wii can update information in all these channels around the clock. You won't have to wait to get today's forecast when you power up your Wii; the forecast should be sitting there waiting for you (**Figure 6.2**).

Figure 6.2
Current weather conditions are available constantly via WiiConnect24.

Setting up WiiConnect24

Setting up WiiConnect24 is a breeze. When your Internet connection is working, follow these steps:

1. Click the Wii Options button in the main screen (**Figure 6.3**).

Figure 6.3
Click the Wii
Options button.

2. Click the Wii Settings icon (**Figure 6.4**) to go to the Wii System Settings screens.

Figure 6.4
Click Wii
Settings.

note The Wii has three System Settings screens (numbered accordingly), and getting from one to the other requires only that you click the arrows on the sides of the screen.

3. Go to the Wii System Settings 2 screen, and click the WiiConnect24 button (**Figure 6.5**).

Figure 6.5
Click
WiiConnect24.

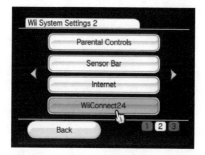

4. In the next screen, click the WiiConnect24 button again (yes, the same button is in two consecutive screens).

You see the WiiConnect24 screen and two options: On and Off.

5. Click On (**Figure 6.6**); then click the Confirm and Back buttons to exit the screen.

That's it. You've turned on the WiiConnect24 service.

Figure 6.6
Click the
On button
to activate
WiiConnect24.

Surfing the Web

The most common activity on the Internet is perusing the World Wide Web. Fortunately for Wii owners, the Internet Channel is a Web browser. Currently in beta form and available for free from the Wii Shop Channel, the Internet Channel Web browser will cost a nominal fee eventually (around 500 to 1,000 Wii Points, or about $5 to $10).

The Opera Web browser powers the Internet Channel. Opera is a slick, functional browser with a start page (**Figure 6.7**) that contains three options: Favorites, Enter a Web Address (WWW), and Help. I explain these three options in the following sections.

Figure 6.7
The start page of the Internet Channel offers three options: Favorites (left), Enter a Web Address (WWW; middle), and Help (right).

Favorites

In the start page, you can click the Favorites button to access the Favorites area (**Figure 6.8**). This area starts out with two preset favorites: the Wii Web page and the Opera Web page.

Figure 6.8
The Favorites area.

To add a Web page to the Favorites area, first click the Favorites button at the bottom of the page (**Figure 6.9**), and then, when you get to the Favorites area, click the Add Favorite button (which has a plus sign on it).

Figure 6.9
Click the Favorites button to go back to the Favorites area, where you can add the last page you looked at to your Favorites list.

tip You can store an unlimited number of Web pages in the Favorites area, but at some point, a large number of pages will become somewhat unwieldy to navigate. I'd say that if you have more than about 18 favorites, you've got too many to scroll through, but that's a matter of opinion.

Enter a Web Address (WWW)

This button takes you to a text-entry screen where you can type a particular Web address that you'd like to go to. This screen (**Figure 6.10**) contains a keyboard with all the letters and symbols you need to access any Web page. Entering an address one keystroke at a time can be a tad cumbersome, but you get used to the process quickly (and can enter most Web addresses quickly too).

Figure 6.10
This screen allows you to enter any Web address.

> **note**
>
> When you're entering a Web address, you don't need to enter **http://** at the beginning. Enter just **www** at the start, and the page will display perfectly.

After you enter the address, click the OK button to bring up that particular page.

To navigate a Web page, press the B button (the trigger on the Wii Remote), and scan the Wii Remote up or down. The remote glides your viewpoint over the Web page in a nice, smooth manner. To zoom in and magnify the text, press the plus (+) key on the remote. Not surprisingly, pressing the minus (–) key zooms back out.

Help

The last button in the start page is Help. Clicking this button brings up a nice graphic of the Wii Remote with an explanation of what each button does in the Opera browser (**Figure 6.11**).

Figure 6.11
To see this image, click the Help button in the Internet Channel's start page.

Setting parental controls

Parents grow concerned when they consider the Internet content their preteen children may have access to. Who can blame them? In fact, I'm one of them.

When it comes to the Wii, some may think that because Nintendo is a family-oriented company, its Internet Channel has built-in filters that prevent users from viewing controversial content, such as pornography. But those people would be dead wrong, because the Internet Channel has no filter at all.

I don't think that the lack of a filter is a bad thing, though, because the Wii has parental controls. These controls (**Figure 6.12**) allow parents to password-protect access to the World Wide Web, the Wii Shop Channel, the News Channel, and Internet Mail—and thereby to control their children's minds as much or as little as their hearts desire.

Figure 6.12
Parental controls let you password-protect various areas of the Wii's services.

To turn on parental controls, follow these steps:

1. Click the Wii Options button in the main screen.

2. Click the Wii Settings icon.

3. Go to the Wii System Settings 2 screen, and click Parental Controls (**Figure 6.13**).

Figure 6.13
Click the Parental Controls button.

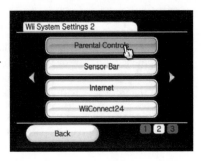

4. If you haven't already done so, set up a password and the question-and-answer pair for retrieving a forgotten password (**Figure 6.14**).

Figure 6.14
Set up your password.

5. After you set a password, click one of the two buttons in the Parental Controls area—Game Settings and PIN, or Other Settings (**Figure 6.15**)—and choose the controls you want to apply.

Figure 6.15
Parental Settings options.

The Game Settings and PIN option lets you change your PIN (personal identification number) and set the highest level of game rating that you will allow the Wii to play without asking for the password (**Figure 6.16**).

Figure 6.16
Use the ESRB (Entertainment Software Rating Board) rating system to set limits on what games your kids can play.

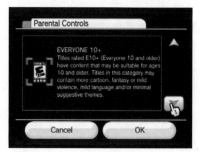

The Other Settings option gives you access to the following yes/no settings (**Figure 6.17**):

* Restrict the use of Wii Points on the Wii Shop Channel?

* Restrict the exchange of mail or other content over WiiConnect24?

* Restrict the use of the Internet Channel?

* Restrict the use of the News Channel?

Figure 6.17
You can restrict activity in four areas, including spending money in the Wii Shop Channel.

Wii-mailing

The last main use of the Wii as an Internet appliance is sending and receiving mail. In the main screen, click the Wii Message Board button; then click the Create Message button in the next screen. From there, you can create messages to send to other registered Wii members (**Figure 6.18**). Currently, you can't send Wii messages to outside email accounts, although I imagine that it won't be long before that feature is available.

Figure 6.18
You can send messages only to registered Wii addresses.

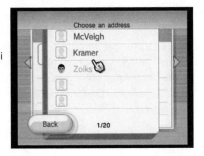

If you want to use a Web-mail service such as Hotmail, Hushmail, or Gmail (any Web-based email service that you access through a browser), you can use regular email to your heart's content via the Opera browser in the Internet Channel.

Wii Belong

The Wii is a fantastic Internet appliance, but it also has some great household uses as a memo taker, a daily organizer, and an exercise machine. (Yes, you read that correctly.) In this section, I look at these areas of usefulness that the Wii offers its owners.

Memos

In the Create Message area of the Wii (which you get to by clicking the Create Message button in the main Wii screen), you find a Memo button. Click the Memo button to reach the memo area, shown in **Figure 6.19,** where you can enter a memo to yourself or others who use your Wii. This memo shows up as mail in the bottom-right corner of the main Wii screen and in the Create Message area; simply click a memo to read it.

Figure 6.19
The memo area.

Calendar

Another tool in the Create Message area is Calendar; to get to it, click the miniature calendar button at the bottom of the screen (**Figure 6.20**). When you click this button, a full-size version of a month-view calendar pops up.

Figure 6.20
The minicalendar button takes you to the Calendar area (go figure).

To move forward or back month by month, use the + and – keys on the Wii Remote. If you want to move forward to 2009 to see what day October 30 is going to fall on, for example, just press the + button enough times to get the calendar up to that month.

One of the great features of Calendar is that you can add memos to any day (past, present, or future) simply by clicking that day, clicking the Memo button, and entering the memo text. It's that simple.

You can put all your key dates—such as birthdays, dinner dates, doctor's appointments, and hair-removal sessions—into Calendar for future reference. Indeed, when you start your Wii and go to the main screen, if Calendar has memos in memory for that day, you see a message icon in the bottom-right corner of the screen, telling you how many memos/messages are waiting for you. Likewise, in calendar view, each day that has a memo attached to

it displays a little envelope to show you that something's up that day (**Figure 6.21**).

Figure 6.21
The month-
view calendar.
Notice the
little envelopes
showing
which days
have memos
attached to
them.

The Helpful Kitty

Every once in a while, you may notice a small cat running along
the top of the Wii's screen. This often happens when you're
waiting for something to load off the Internet—when the News
Channel is loading, for example. If you click this little cat, you get
a tip about some aspect of using the Wii (**Figure 6.22**). What tip
you get is random, but this feature is a cute and fun way to get
little tidbits of information.

Figure 6.22
Clicking the cat
causes a tip to
appear.

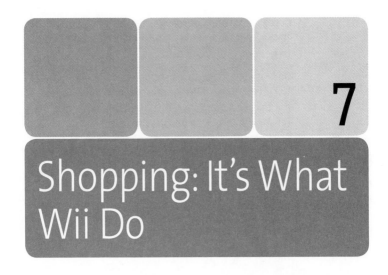

7

Shopping: It's What Wii Do

Not to worry, fearless shopping warriors—the Wii can satisfy your shopping needs. The Wii Shop Channel (**Figure 7.1**) stands ready to satiate you with

Figure 7.1
The Wii Shop Channel is ready to meet all your Virtual Console spending needs.

oodles of Virtual Console games designed not only to take you down memory lane, but also to entice you to get out your credit cards.

Because Nintendo takes shopping seriously enough to create a separate shopping channel, it behooves me to take a quick look at the various forms of buying you can accomplish with a Wii.

Shop Channel Reliability

Many people worry about shopping online with their credit cards. This feeling may stem in part from fear of sending personal information into the void, where some nefarious character could take advantage of it. More often than not, though, folks are just afraid that their purchases will fail in some way and that they'll end up losing their money with no recourse.

Today's online stores are hyper-reliable, however. I can tell you that from the day that my kids started bugging me to buy Virtual Console software, I had no problems with any aspect of the Wii Shop Channel—using Wii Points Cards, buying Wii Points with a credit card, and generally putting the entire site through its paces without a single hiccup.

Shopping the Wii Shop Channel

The Wii Shop Channel is included with the Wii and ready to go as soon as the device is powered up and connected to the Internet. As I mention in Chapter 3, this channel contains two main stores: Virtual Console and Wii Ware. Although the Virtual Console store is there to sell you a plethora of out-of-circulation games for the likes of the Sega Genesis and TurboGrafx 16, the Wii Ware store is designed to be the portal to new Wii Channels as they are released.

Using Wii Points Cards

Tradable currency in the Wii realm consists of special units called *Wii Points*. You can get these points in two ways: by purchasing a prepaid Wii Points Card from an electronics or gaming store, or by purchasing the points in the Wii Shop Channel with a credit card.

Wii Points Cards are available only in 2,000-point denominations for around $20 ($25 Canadian). It doesn't take a rocket scientist to see that each U.S. dollar is worth roughly 100 Wii Points, so a game that costs 500 Wii Points has a real-world cost of $5.

note

Nintendo doesn't plan to issue Wii Points Cards in any denomination other than 2,000 points—at least, not in North America. But 5,000-point cards are available in Japan, so perhaps different Wii Points Card denominations will appear over time.

Redeeming a Wii Points Card

If you purchased a Wii Points Card or got one as a gift, follow these steps to redeem it:

1. In the main Wii screen, click the Wii Shop Channel's TV-screen icon to get into the Wii Shop Channel (**Figure 7.2**); then click Start Shopping.

Figure 7.2
When you're in the Wii Shop Channel, click Start Shopping.

2. Click the Add Wii Points button (**Figure 7.3**).

Figure 7.3
Click Add Wii Points.

3. In the Add Wii Points screen, click Redeem Wii Points Card (**Figure 7.4**).

Figure 7.4
Click the Redeem Wii Points Card button.

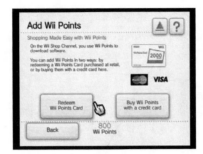

4. In the Redeem Wii Points Card screen, click the activation-number box (**Figure 7.5**).

You go to a screen with a numeric keypad where you can enter the Wii Points Card Activation Number. (This number is on the back of the Wii Points Card; to reveal it, scratch off the opaque plastic coating.)

Figure 7.5
Click the activation-number box.

5. To cash in your points, enter the activation number (**Figure 7.6**) and then click the OK button.

Figure 7.6
Enter your number (this one isn't real, so don't bother trying to duplicate it); then click OK.

Buying Wii Points with a credit card

The other way to get Wii Points is to buy them in the Wii Shop Channel with your credit card and add the points to your account directly. To do this, first complete steps 1 and 2 of "Redeeming a Wii Points Card" to get to the Add Wii Points screen. Then follow these steps:

1. Click Buy Wii Points with a Credit Card (**Figure 7.7**).

Figure 7.7
Click the Buy Wii Points button.

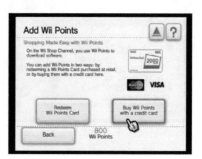

You enter the Wii Points Purchase screen, where you can choose among point values ranging from 1,000 to 5,000. I'll save you the trouble of doing the simple math: There's no advantage to buying more points, because the cost is the same regardless. (Darn it!)

2. Pick the amount you want to buy and then click that button (**Figure 7.8**).

Figure 7.8
Choose the amount of points you want.

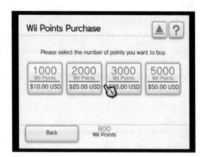

3. Choose your payment method (**Figure 7.9**): MasterCard or Visa (sorry, Amex and Discover).

Figure 7.9
Choose which credit card you want to use to pay.

4. In the next screen, enter the card number, expiration date, and security code (**Figure 7.10**).

Figure 7.10
Enter the
pertinent
credit-card
information.

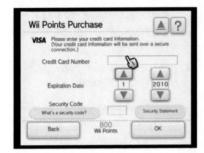

5. Enter the abbreviation for the province or state you live in, plus your postal or zip code (**Figure 7.11**); then click OK.

Figure 7.11
Finish the
information
for credit-card
verification.

6. In the Wii Points Purchase Confirmation screen, verify the number of points you're purchasing, and confirm or cancel the purchase (**Figure 7.12**).

Figure 7.12
Confirm or kill
the purchase by
clicking the Yes
or No button.

7. After authorizing the purchase, you get a screen
   that shows how many points you just purchased
   and your current point balance (**Figure 7.13**); click
   OK to close the screen.

Figure 7.13
You get an
initial receipt
that shows your
purchase and
current point
balance.

note Clicking the View Receipt button (which is in the
screen that appears immediately after authorization)
shows you a detailed receipt that looks a lot like the
MasterCard and Visa receipts you receive in most stores.

Making a Virtual Console purchase

The Virtual Console includes all kinds of games for the Nintendo Entertainment System (NES), the Super Nintendo Entertainment System (SNES), the Nintendo 64 (N64), the Sega Genesis, and the TurboGrafx 16 systems. All these old systems run perfectly in emulation on the Wii, making it possible for you to enjoy these games just like you did 10 or even 20 years ago.

Whether you're dying to get your hands on some old Genesis game that you used to love, or your kids are bugging the heck out of you to purchase some old Mario game from the SNES days (as my kids do), it probably won't be long before you end up purchasing a Virtual Console title via the Wii. Make sure that you've got some Wii Points ready to spend, fire up the Wii Shop Channel, and follow these steps:

1. Click the Virtual Console button (**Figure 7.14**).

Figure 7.14
Click Virtual
Console to get
started.

2. In the Virtual Console store, specify how you want to view the games: by system, by title in alphabetical order, or by date of addition to the store (which means that the newest additions to the store show up first).

For this exercise, click the Show Games from One Game System button (**Figure 7.15**).

Figure 7.15
Click Show Games from One Game System.

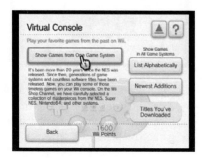

3. Click the gaming system you want to find a game for (**Figure 7.16**).

The Wii Shop Channel displays a list of games.

Figure 7.16
Choose the game system that interests you.

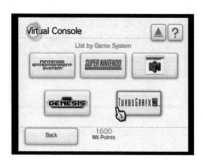

4. Click the game that you want to see in more detail in the Details screen (**Figure 7.17**).

Figure 7.17
The Details screen for Bomberman '93, a TurboGrafx 16 game.

If you want to learn a *lot* more about the game, click the More Details button in the bottom-right corner; you get a highly detailed description of the game, complete with screen shots (**Figure 7.18**). When you're done, click Back to return to the Details screen.

Figure 7.18
The More Details area gives you a long description and screen shots of the game.

5. If you decide that you want the game, click the Download button in the Details screen.

6. In the Download Confirmation screen, click Yes to purchase and download the software (**Figure 7.19**).

Figure 7.19
This screen is your final chance to back out if you change your mind.

After you click Yes, you move to the Download Software screen (**Figure 7.20**), where the download begins immediately. You get to watch either Mario or Luigi running across the screen picking up coins as the download proceeds. Downloads tend to take less than a minute with a high-speed connection.

Figure 7.20
The download process is speedy most times. After all, old games aren't big.

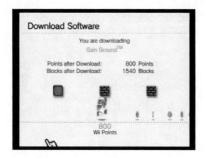

When the download is complete, a confirmation screen shows you how many blocks of memory the game occupies and how many blocks remain for future storage, plus how many Wii Points you have left.

When you move to the Wii's main screen, the game you purchased appears as one of the channels, as shown in **Figure 7.21**. To play the game, simply click its newly activated channel.

Figure 7.21
Each down-loaded Virtual Console game shows up in the main Wii screen as its own channel.

Virtual Console Prices

The prices of Virtual Console titles vary according to the consoles on which the games were released originally. The following list shows you exactly how many Wii Points (and the equivalent U.S. dollars) a single game for each system costs:

- NES: 500 points ($5)
- SNES: 600 points ($6)
- Sega Genesis: 800 points ($8)
- TurboGrafx 16: 800 points ($8)
- N64: 1,000 points ($10)

The prices are reasonable, considering that these games are fully functional, with no control problems (that is, the controllers work perfectly even though the games are several generations behind current technology) and with multiplayer capabilities in games that originally had them.

Buying Wii Ware

The Wii Ware store (**Figure 7.22**) is the place to download—and in some cases, purchase—new Wii Channels. At this writing, the Everybody Votes Channel is available free through the Wii Ware store, and so is the trial version of the Internet Channel. When the Internet Channel software is finalized and all features are in place, however, you'll pay a small price to download the new version (probably 500 to 1,000 Wii Points, or $5 to $10).

Figure 7.22
The Wii Ware area is the access point for new Wii Channels.

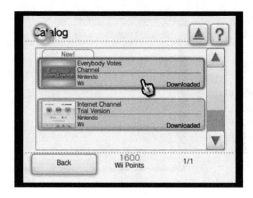

Checking Your Account Activity

After you use your Wii Points a fair bit, and you get into the habit of adding points via a Wii Points Card or direct purchase, you should go to the Account Activity screen (**Figure 7.23**) to see exactly what has been going into and out of your account. This screen is a great way to see what you (and other members of your family) are buying with your money.

To get to the Account Activity screen, click the Account Activity button in the main screen of the Wii Shop Channel (refer to Figure 7.3 earlier in this chapter).

Figure 7.23
The Account Activity screen is a handy way to get an overview of your activities in the Wii Shop Channel.

Date	Type	Content	Wii Points	Current Point Balance
02/19/07	Wii Points Purchase	Credit Card	+3,000	3,800
02/19/07	Software Download	Gain Ground™	-800	800
02/14/07	Software Download	Everybody Votes	0	1,600
02/14/07	Software Download	Super Mario Bros.™	-500	1,600

Back   3800 Wii Points   1/3

Shopping on the Internet

The Wii Shop Channel is a great place, but it carries a limited assortment of items. Heck, you can't even buy Wii accessories there (yet). If you want to do serious online shopping, you need to head over to the Internet Channel and use the Opera browser to do your shopping, just as you would on your computer (**Figure 7.24**).

Figure 7.24
Shopping on Amazon.com with the Wii's Opera browser.

Online shopping with the Wii is simplicity itself. Simply find the product you want, select it, and enter your address and credit-card numbers; the seller gladly takes your money. A few days (or weeks) later, the product shows up in your mailbox, and everyone's happy.

tip When you shop on the Internet, make sure that you are dealing with a reputable Web site, such as Amazon.com or Etsy.com. Always verify that your transaction is secure. (A small lock icon appears in secure transactions, and the words *secure transaction* usually appear as well.)

8

A-Gaming Wii Will Go

Sure, the Wii has a progressive, cutting-edge control system. Sure, it includes some great software that personalizes the Wii experience. And sure, it's brilliantly positioned as a useful Internet appliance that anyone in the family can use to communicate, shop, or check the weather. But even though the Wii can do all these things, its fundamental purpose is to play games.

The Wii doesn't play just any games—it plays great games and, in some cases, groundbreaking games (mostly due to the unique wireless controller system). The Wii can work in a backward-compatible mode to play Nintendo GameCube games and lots of old-time games through the Virtual Console, as well as modern Wii-specific games. In this chapter, I look at all these types of games.

What to Look for in a Wii Game

When you go to a store to pick out Wii games, look for a few key features:

- **Multiplayer capability.** Although many games are lots of fun to play by yourself, playing with or against a friend or relative gives a game another dimension to explore and enjoy.

- **Controllers.** Make sure that you have the controllers needed to play the game. Some games require two Wii Remotes with Nunchuks, for example.

- **Appropriateness.** If your children are going to be playing the game, be sure that the content is appropriate for their ages. Also be sure to read the cover notes to ensure that the content doesn't conflict with your belief system. I once loaned an unopened game called The Vampire's Masquerade to a friend, and he returned it in the same state a few days later. When I asked him why he hadn't opened the game, he said his wife felt that the content encouraged Satanism. Everybody is entitled to his or her own beliefs, and that's why I encourage you to educate yourself about games before buying them.

- **Strategy guides.** For some games, such as Zelda, you may want to see whether a strategy guide is available. These books tell you how to beat the game and give you inside tips and tricks about the gaming universe. If you get frustrated with games easily, it might behoove you to pick up a strategy guide. Some strategy guides are also available online at no cost.

- **Rating.** If you have visited gaming sites, you may have seen ratings for certain games. These ratings are not always in line with what your opinion is going to be when you play the game, but they're a reasonable approximation.

- **Popularity.** If a game is flying off the shelves and is not in stock anywhere, you can get a pretty good idea that the game is a good one. Buying a game on the basis of popularity alone is foolish, but taken with the other factors, a game's popularity is worth considering.

Online Game Information

Rating and comparing games is much like rating and comparing movies; one man's *The Godfather* is another man's *Dude, Where's My Car?* Still, most gamers accept a basic division line that puts games in either the good or the not-so-good category, which is where gaming Web sites come into the picture.

(continues on next page)

Online Game Information (continued)

All kinds of Web sites review games and accessories for the Wii, but the following are probably the top five places to visit:

- IGN.com (http://wii.ign.com)
- GameSpot (www.gamespot.com; click the Wii button)
- Wikipedia (http://en.wikipedia.org/wiki/List_of_Wii_games)
- Yahoo Games (http://wii.yahoo.com)
- Wii.com (http://wii.com)

These sites have exhaustive lists of Wii games (**Figure 8.1**), reviews of already-released games, and even previews of games that are not yet released.

Figure 8.1
IGN.com's Wii coverage is extensive.

Many gaming sites also have videos of in-game action, strategy guides, cheats, codes, reader reviews, interviews with the game's designers, and lots of other ancillary material to feed your interest in the game in question. Ultimately, the Web is a powerful tool for you to use when deciding where to spend your hard-earned money.

The Best Wii Games

New Wii games are being released every week, so my giving you a complete, detailed picture of all the available games is impossible. But I can give you a picture of what's good right now, as I write this chapter.

In this section, I look at six of the top games on the market—games that take full advantage of the Wii's control system and are likely to go down in the history books as classic entertainment software (**Figure 8.2**). This collection includes two sports games, a sprawling adventure, a car-racing game, an action game, and two crazy family games that are more fun than a clown on fire.

Figure 8.2
Here's a cross-section of great games to start with on the Wii.

note

ESRB (Entertainment Software Rating Board) standards came into practice in 1994. A volunteer effort by software producers in the United States and Canada, the ESRB rating system helps parents choose appropriate software for their children.

GT Pro Series

Genre: Car racing
Publisher: Ubisoft
Price: $49.99
ESRB rating: E (Everyone)
Multiplayer? No
Controllers needed: Wii Remote

GT Pro Series (**Figure 8.3**) is the only game I'm recommending that doesn't get a high rating from the major gaming sites. I like GT Pro Series because it includes a free racing wheel (see Chapter 9 for details on this accessory) and is easy enough for a 5-year-old to play.

Figure 8.3
GT Pro Series isn't a cutting-edge racing game, but it's fun for beginners.

The Legend of Zelda: Twilight Princess

Genre: Adventure
Publisher: Nintendo
Price: $49.99
ESRB rating: T (Teen)
Multiplayer? No
Controllers needed: Wii Remote + Nunchuk

Zelda (**Figure 8.4**) is one of the most beloved gaming franchises of all time, and Twilight Princess doesn't disappoint. It's a complex, engrossing game that's still easy enough for an 8-year-old to follow (if you allow an 8-year-old to play a T-rated game), and it's all kinds of fun. The puzzles are enjoyable and challenging, the graphics are pleasing, and the controls (as expected) are out of this world.

Figure 8.4
Twilight Princess lives up to the high expectations of Zelda fans.

Madden NFL 07

Genre: American football
Publisher: EA SPORTS
Price: $49.99
ESRB rating: E (Everyone)
Multiplayer? Yes (up to four players)
Controllers needed: Wii Remote + Nunchuk

The Madden series is by far the most popular football gaming series *ever,* and the Wii version opens the door to many gamers who find the controls in other versions too difficult to master. In Madden NFL 07 (**Figure 8.5**), you throw a ball by making a throwing motion (a large flick of the wrist), and you snap the ball from center by jerking up the Wii Remote. This game is a great deal of fun.

Figure 8.5
Madden NFL 07 takes full advantage of the Wii's unique wireless control system.

Rayman Raving Rabbids

Genre: This game defies description!
Publisher: Ubisoft
Price: $49.99
ESRB rating: E (Everyone)
Multiplayer? Yes (up to four players)
Controllers needed: Wii Remote + Nunchuk

Rayman Raving Rabbids (**Figure 8.6**) is one of the most hilarious games I've ever played. The game takes brilliant advantage of the Wii's controllers, and the bizarre story is frighteningly compelling. Before you know it, you'll be shooting bathroom plungers at cowboy rabbits and then flying a giant bat to pick up a pig and drop it into a farmyard.

Figure 8.6
Rayman Raving Rabbids is outrageous fun, plain and simple.

If all that seems strange, be prepared to drum along to all kinds of music (a missed drumbeat can mean death) and then engage in the world-famous cow toss. Yep, you read that right: You grab a cow, spin it round and round over your head, and then release it to see how far you can get it to go. (The cow is often unimpressed.)

Rayman Raving Rabbids is quite simply one of the finest family games out there for any console. It's great fun for all ages and a personal favorite of mine.

Red Steel

Genre: First-person action
Publisher: Ubisoft
Price: $49.99
ESRB rating: T (Teen)
Multiplayer? Yes (up to four players)
Controllers needed: Wii Remote + Nunchuk

Red Steel (**Figure 8.7**) definitely contains adult themes, the worst of which are violence and onscreen killing. You have to fight your way through detailed and realistic areas, using various weapons—guns, automatic weapons, and even ninja swords. Parts of the game can be a real workout (especially the swordfighting). Getting used to the controls takes a while, but after you do, the game's a lot of fun.

Figure 8.7
You need both the Wii Remote and the Nunchuk to play Red Steel.

Wario Ware: Smooth Moves

Genre: Microgames
Publisher: Nintendo
Price: $49.99
ESRB rating: E (Everyone; age 10 and up recommended)
Multiplayer? No
Controllers needed: Wii Remote + Nunchuk

Wario Ware: Smooth Moves (**Figure 8.8**) nearly defies categorization. The idea is that you must move through a map and defeat hundreds of microgames to win. No other game uses the Wii Remote in so many ways; the diversity of uses for the remote is truly impressive.

Figure 8.8
Wario Ware is a ton of fun for kids and adults alike. Anyone who wants to learn every nuance of the Wii Remote should play this game for an hour.

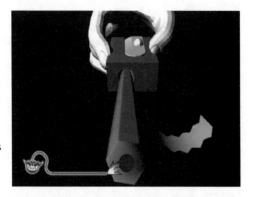

Despite the remarkable simplicity of the graphics and the microgames, Smooth Moves is highly compelling, and I recommend it as a fantastic single-player game for the whole family. That may seem like an oxymoron, but Smooth Moves lends itself to a group of people taking turns against the microgames.

Backward Compatibility

The Wii is a great gaming platform, with plenty of games already available for it, and no doubt hundreds more will be available in the coming months and years. Add to that the plethora of Virtual Console games and the backward compatibility of Nintendo GameCube games, and the Wii becomes a true all-in-one system.

note

Backward compatibility simply means that a console is capable of playing games created for earlier consoles. Sony PlayStation 3, for example, can play all PlayStation games to date. The Nintendo GameCube isn't backward compatible, because the Nintendo 64 (the console that preceded it) uses a cartridge system, whereas the GameCube uses discs. But the Wii's disc drive makes it backward compatible with the GameCube.

Wii users can rejoice: Not only are all GameCube games compatible with the Wii (indeed, the Wii has four GameCube controller slots and two memory-card slots), but also, the Wii's Virtual Console provides access to many other old games.

In this section, I look at a few standout GameCube and Virtual Console titles.

note

So many fantastic games are available through the Virtual Console that pretty much any one you pick will be a winner. Let's face it—the games that make it into the Virtual Console are the ones that were good sellers 10, 15, and 20 years ago, so all of them should be good.

Virtual Console

The Wii Shop Channel (covered in Chapter 7) gives you access to large numbers of old games for the Nintendo Entertainment System (NES), Super Nintendo Entertainment System (SNES), Nintendo 64 (N64), Sega Genesis, and TurboGrafx systems through the Virtual Console (**Figure 8.9**). The following sections describe three of the best Virtual Console titles currently available.

Figure 8.9
The Wii's Virtual Console.

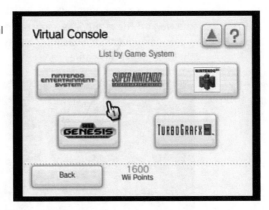

tip   When you go to Web sites such as IGN.com's Wii area, the old games available through the Virtual Console are newly rated, which allows you to get a fresh perspective on whether various games are worth their cost.

Super Mario 64

Genre: Platformer
Publisher: Nintendo
Price: 1,000 Wii Points ($10)
ESRB rating: E (Everyone)
Multiplayer? No
Controllers needed: Classic Controller or GameCube controller

Super Mario 64 (**Figure 8.10**) is one of the all-time best games, single-handedly responsible for getting the N64 off the ground. As a matter of fact, many gamers bought their N64s just so they could get their hands on this game.

Figure 8.10
Super Mario 64 is a classic.

Super Mario World

Genre: Platformer
Publisher: Nintendo
Price: 600 Wii Points ($6)
ESRB rating: E (Everyone)
Multiplayer? Yes
Controllers needed: Classic Controller or GameCube controller

Super Mario World (**Figure 8.11**) is a side-scrolling platform game from about a thousand years ago—and amazingly, it holds my children's interest. Even though the kids have access to some of the best games on the planet, they're more than willing to spend an hour on this one.

Figure 8.11
It's old, but Super Mario World is still great.

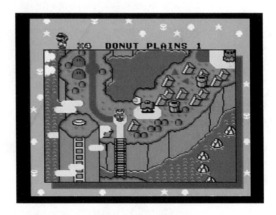

ToeJam & Earl

Genre: Action/adventure
Publisher: Sega
Price: 800 Wii Points ($8)
ESRB rating: E (Everyone)
Multiplayer? Yes
Controllers needed: Classic Controller or GameCube controller

The concept of ToeJam & Earl (**Figure 8.12**) is that the characters have crash-landed on a funkified planet, and now their spaceship is in a bunch of pieces. They must explore the planet and recover the ten ship pieces necessary to get off the world and get home. ToeJam & Earl is a peculiar game, but it's surprisingly fun and a great two-player game for kids.

Figure 8.12
An odd game when it came out, ToeJam & Earl is still odd—but also a lot of fun.

Operations Guides

When you are playing a Virtual Console game, you may wonder what you are supposed to do for a manual—which you don't get when you download a game through the Wii Shop Channel.

Complete manuals are included with every Virtual Console game. To get a manual while you're playing one of these games, just press the Home button on the Wii Remote and then click the Operations Guide button. The Wii displays the Operations Guide (manual) for the game you are playing. **Figure 8.13** shows Super Mario 64's Operations Guide.

Figure 8.13
Operations Guides are complete manuals included with every Virtual Console game.

GameCube games

Tons of GameCube games are available (some of them available for a song at game-trading stores), and the GameCube is still for sale everywhere, so it's safe to say that GameCube games are still in development. Because the Wii is backward compatible, all GameCube games are available to you. I suggest that you visit Web sites such as GameSpot and IGN.com to read about games before you buy them.

The following sections discuss just a few of the games in the venerable GameCube catalog.

Lego Star Wars II: The Original Trilogy

Genre: Action/adventure
Publisher: LucasArts
Price: $39.99
ESRB rating: E (Everybody)
Multiplayer? Yes (cooperative)
Controllers needed: Classic Controllers or GameCube controllers

Lego Star Wars II (**Figure 8.14**) is one of the most surprisingly enjoyable games of recent years. The game features all the *Star Wars* characters (in Lego form) and leaves you to take them through the entire story arc of the original *Star Wars* movie and its sequels, *The Empire Strikes Back* (Episode V) and *Return of the Jedi* (Episode VI)—the first three movies from way back in the 1970s and early 1980s.

Figure 8.14
Lego Star Wars II is one of the most surprising (in a good way) games of the past few years.

I can't say enough just how much fun this game is. The cooperative multiplayer feature is a blast, and I've spent countless hours with both of my sons working through the game as the likes of Obi-Wan, R2-D2, and even Chewbacca.

Luigi's Mansion

Genre: Action/adventure
Publisher: Nintendo
Price: $9 (used)
ESRB rating: E (Everyone)
Multiplayer? No
Controllers needed: Classic Controller or GameCube controller

Luigi's Mansion (**Figure 8.15**) puts its protagonist in a haunted mansion that's chock full of ghosts and other annoying spirits. Luigi must use his handy-dandy ghost vacuum to suck up the enemies while he works to find his way out of the mansion.

Figure 8.15
A great classic with ghosts, Luigi's Mansion is lots of fun for younger kids.

Super Smash Bros. Melee

Genre: Action/fighting
Publisher: Nintendo
Price: $29.99
ESRB rating: T (Teen)
Multiplayer? Yes
Controllers needed: Classic Controllers or GameCube controllers

Super Smash Bros. Melee (**Figure 8.16**) takes the main characters from famous Nintendo games such as Link from Zelda, Mario and Luigi, Bowser, Princess Peach, and even Samus from Metroid, and puts them in an all-out fight in a variety of settings. Although Super Smash Bros. is a fighting game, there's no real violence—more like cartoon fun. The game has no recognizable weapons, violent actions, blood, gore, or anything else that most parents would consider inappropriate.

Figure 8.16
A classic among kids, Super Smash Bros. Melee pits the main characters from many Nintendo games against one another.

Wii Accessories

Accessories for a gaming console usually start as a relatively small trickle of items. As the unit gains in popularity, and as certain needs are discovered or games that require a special accessory are developed, that trickle becomes a raging torrent of products. At this writing, the Wii has been on the market for only a few months and has a relatively small selection of accessories. You can be sure that the list is going to grow to iPod-accessories level within the next 12 months.

In this chapter, I look at a few of the most important Wii accessories currently on the market.

Protection and Beauty

Plenty of accessories are available to protect and beautify the Wii and its components, including the Wii Remote and the accessory controllers. This section shows you the most interesting and useful items in this group.

Skins

Skins (covers) for any console system fall into two categories:

- **Protective.** These skins protect the objects they cover, guarding them against dirt, scratches, and (in some cases) the shock of being dropped.

- **Decorative.** These skins are purely aesthetic, appealing only to vanity. They include peel-on (and peel-off) stickers or decals that can turn the Wii into a temporary work of art.

Protective skins

One type of skin that's important to Wii users is the protective type. The skins placed on Wii Remotes and Nunchuks usually are made out of silicon, and they provide a significant measure of overall protection. Many people, however, like to use a skin on their remotes specifically for the feel the skin gives them. Indeed, a skin gives you a nice strong grip on a Wii Remote, making you feel as though the remote couldn't fly out of your hands even if you wanted it to.

I use Mad Catz SKINZ (**Figure 9.1**; www.madcatz.com) on my Wii Remotes, and I'm very happy with them.

But you can find skins from other manufacturers, such as Intec, and plenty of no-name-brand skins sell on Amazon.com and eBay for less than $10 each.

Figure 9.1
A skin on a Wii Remote is not only functional, but looks great as well.

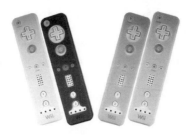

Decorative skins

Several Web sites sell decorative skins for the Wii console. These skins (**Figure 9.2**) are actually precision decals made with a very cool technology that allows you to put the decal on and then peel it off at any time without damaging, altering, or marking up your Wii at all.

To see a selection of these skins, go to www.decalgirl. com or www.designerskins.com. Both sites offer an outstanding selection of skins to trick out your Wii.

Figure 9.2
You can find lots of cool skins for the Wii online.

Wrist straps

Due to the hullabaloo about the supposed fragility of the original Wii Remote wrist straps, several companies have come out with their own reinforced wrist straps. Mad Catz now offers wrist straps, as does ASID Tech (www.asidtech.com), and no doubt many more strap choices will be on the market in the very near future.

Currently, all the replacement straps are generic, with the only real variance being the colors of the straps. If you're looking for a new wrist strap, I suggest waiting for something that's really cool. Down the road, someone's bound to release a strap that is special in some way, so keep your eyes open.

Functional Accessories

Although wrist straps and skins are useful accessories, they fall into the "vanity" category as far as I'm concerned. The accessories in this section—ranging from battery chargers to AV cables—tend to be more functional and serve a specific function on the Wii.

Intec G5615 Wii Vertical Stand

I'll be honest and tell you that I wasn't too crazy about the vertical stand that came with my Wii, because my kids managed to topple the console three times during its first day of use. I calculated that if that kept happening, especially while the disc drive was in use, my Wii would be junk in a hurry.

As a result, I went out to a local store and found an Intec Wii Vertical Stand (**Figure 9.3**). This little puppy has cradle spots for GameCube memory cards, two Wii Remotes, two Nunchuks, and even an extra SD card. In short, it's a great (and stable) vertical stand for the Wii.

Figure 9.3
At $15.99, the Intec G5615 Wii Vertical Stand is a solid deal.

note Why is it so easy sometimes to topple a Wii that's mounted in a vertical stand? Many Wii owners like the old GameCube controllers, so when they play their GameCube titles, they plug the GameCube controllers into the top of the Wii. If those controllers get tugged just the wrong way, the walls come tumblin' down, so to speak.

Intec Wii Pro Gamer's Case

Intec has made a habit of coming up with cool-looking metallic carrying cases for nearly every gaming platform on the planet, and the Nintendo Wii is no exception. The Wii Pro Gamer's Case (**Figure 9.4**) usually sells for $29.99; it includes separate compartments for controllers, cables, games, and nearly anything else you want to tote along. The aluminum case is solid, and everything fits inside snugly so that it doesn't rattle around and become damaged in transit. Although this sort of case is excellent for in-home storage, it really shines when you need to take your Wii to a new location.

Figure 9.4
Intec's case protects your Wii gear from most home and road hazards.

note Although an aluminum case looks great and is a fantastic way to tote your Wii around, it tends to raise red flags in an airport security lineup. If you plan to take a metal game case on a plane as carry-on luggage, you may have a bit of a delay in the security area.

Nintendo Component AV cable

When I found out that the Wii is not capable of high-definition output, what I said isn't repeatable here, but suffice it to say that it sounded at least a little bit like "Dagnab it!" Those of us who wanted HD with our Wiis are out of luck, but the Wii can still generate output in 480p mode (see the "Progressive Scan" sidebar in this section), which means that the picture, though not higher in definition, is clearer and more stable than a traditional television picture.

Even though you can't have the real HD deal, you can have progressive scan with your Wii—as long as you have a Component AV cable (**Figure 9.5**). As it happens, you can get one from Nintendo.com for $29.95.

Figure 9.5
If you want to enjoy progressive-scan output, you need a Component AV cable with the video output spit into three jacks, like this one from Nintendo.

Progressive Scan

Although the Wii isn't capable of HD output, it *can* output in progressive-scan mode at 480p. What the heck is 480p, and why should you care?

First, to enjoy 480p output, you must have a television set that's capable of displaying that output. If your TV has what's called a Component input, it's capable of displaying 480p. A Component input typically has five connectors—two for audio and three for the video signal. Component inputs break the video signal into three separate channels (usually coded red, green, and blue) rather than a single Composite or S-Video input. The audio portion of the cable has two jacks for sound (a left and a right channel).

So what does 480p mean? A TV screen displays a series of horizontal lines that are drawn 30 times a second, but instead of drawing every single line on every pass, the TV set draws every *second* line on one pass and the missing lines on the next pass. The result is that you can sometimes see a TV set flicker. Another giveaway is the fact that if you try to videotape a program playing on a TV set, you see a big line moving up the screen. This line is created because the screen is being drawn one half at a time. The drawing happens so quickly that the human eye can't detect it; we interpret the image as a whole image.

A TV that produces 480p output draws every line 60 times a second, so the image is drawn completely every single time it's painted on the screen. For this reason, 480p images appear to be a little brighter and more stable, although the difference isn't nearly as dramatic as the difference with HD signals. Still, if you've got 480p capability, you may as well take advantage of it.

Battery chargers

ASID Tech (www.asidtech.com) recently announced that it's producing a Wii Charge Station (**Figure 9.6**) that lets Wii owners use battery packs to power their Wii Remotes instead of expensive AA batteries. The Wii Charge Station is powered by the Wii's USB port, so you don't need another wall outlet to plug in the charger; just turn the Wii on and put a battery pack in the charger to recharge it. If you use your remote extensively, a battery-charger system like this one may be worthwhile.

Figure 9.6
ASID Tech's Wii Charge Station.

Another manufacturer, dreamGEAR (www. dreamgear.net), has announced a similar battery-charger kit.

Nintendo Wi-Fi USB Connector

This device (**Figure 9.7**) allows you to connect the Wii to the Internet wirelessly through a Windows-based computer that's connected to the Internet. Check out Chapter 2 for details on how to set up the connector. The unit costs $29.99, and considering what it does, it's priced fairly.

Figure 9.7
The Nintendo Wi-Fi USB Connector works very well.

Nintendo Wii LAN Adapter

Not yet released (but announced), this connector is designed to connect your Wii to the Internet via a standard Ethernet cable. Until the product is actually on the shelf, I won't know how it works, but I assume that because it's a Nintendo-branded product, it's going to work fine.

You can preorder the Wii LAN Adapter at Nintendo's Web site (www.nintendo.com/consumer/systems/wii/en_na/acc/wiiLAN.jsp) for $24.99.

Wii Sports Pack controller adapters

Plenty of interesting Wii Remote adapters are showing up, including the Wii Sports Pack from Joytech (currently selling only in Europe, but you can still order it in North America by placing an order via the Internet). The Sports Pack (**Figure 9.8**) includes a tennis racquet, a steering wheel, and a miniature golf club. These items are just fun props that make playing the Wii Sports games more fun, but for many gamers who lack finesse with controllers, these add-ons can help a great deal.

Figure 9.8
Joytech's Wii Sports Pack has a comical look, with its miniature controllers.

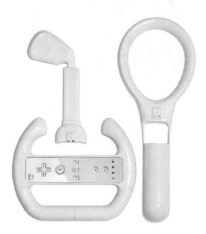

Ubisoft Wii steering wheel

This steering wheel (**Figure 9.9**) comes with Ubisoft's GT Pro Series racing game (but it can be purchased separately from Ubisoft as well). As simple as this device looks, it's amazing how much it adds to the enjoyment of racing a car on the Wii. When you start "driving" with the steering wheel, you quickly forget that you're holding a videogame controller. You believe that you're holding a real car's wheel—no joke.

Figure 9.9
The author holding the Ubisoft steering wheel.

SD Cards

SD Memory Cards (*SD* stands for *secure digital*) are flash memory cards used in a variety of portable devices, such as cameras, camcorders, cell phones, MP3 players, and even the Wii. In fact, the SD card is the only storage option currently available for the Wii. The cards are inexpensive, and they come in sizes from 128 MB right up to 2 GB. I purchased a pair of 1 GB SD cards for my Wii, and even with the purchase (and subsequent saving) of many Virtual Console games, I haven't come close to using up that first gigabyte of memory.

If you don't have a PC, camera, or MP3 player with an SD card slot, you can solve this problem in a very inexpensive way. One good solution is to get a USB card reader like the Belkin Hi-Speed USB 2.0 15-in-1 Media Reader/Writer ($39.99 at www.belkin.com).

Many other media-card readers are available for a lot less money, however. I dug around my computer room and found an older Belkin card reader (**Figure 9.10**) that plugs into a USB port; it reads and writes on SD cards straight up, and I don't even need to add software to my Windows or Mac computer. (Most card readers don't require additional software, so they are dead simple to use.) When you plug your SD card into your computer, it shows up on your computer as a portable hard drive, not unlike a portable USB drive.

Figure 9.10
My old-fashioned Belkin media-card reader still works like a charm.

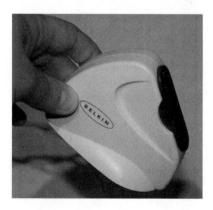

Nintendo decided to make SD cards the only media for getting files on and off the Wii, so if you want to save game files, view photos on the Wii, or even move music to the Wii, you *must* understand how to get files on and off SD cards. Fortunately, using these cards with your computer and the Wii is very simple; the only problem is finding an inexpensive card reader. For your convenience, here are a few inexpensive but effective media-card readers:

- SanDisk ImageMate 12-in-1 USB 2.0 Hi-Speed Reader (www.sandisk.com; $29.99)

- Kingston Technology USB 2.0 Hi-Speed 15-in-1 Reader (www.kingston.com; $19.99)

- Lexar Media USB 2.0 12-in-1 Reader (www.lexar.com; $39.99)

- SimpleTech Multi-Card Reader Adapter 4-1 (www.simpletech.com; $26.99)

Transferring Music and Photos

As I mention in Chapter 3, you can use SD cards to transfer MP3 music files and digital photographs to and from your Wii. Because SD cards are often used in digital cameras, and because some PCs have built-in SD card readers, it made sense to put an SD card reader in the Wii (and Nintendo did).

To put MP3 files or digital photographs on an SD card, simply plug the card into your computer and copy the files to the card. When the files are in place, take the SD card back to your Wii, plug it in, and go to the Photo Channel. The Wii reads your photos immediately (**Figure 9.11**).

Figure 9.11
When the SD card is back in the Wii, the pictures show up without a hitch.

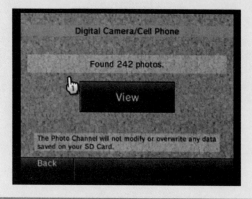

10

Wii Mods and Hacks

When a new gaming console arrives on the market, it usually doesn't take long for various mods and hacks to hit the streets. *Mods* is short for *modifications,* and *hacks* are modifications that aren't sanctioned by the console's manufacturer. Manufacturers rarely appreciate or sanction mods and hacks. Still, some companies show a tacit acceptance of some mods and hacks because they often help make a console more popular and give it more functionality.

Because the Wii hasn't been on the market long, limited modifications and few true hacks are currently available, but that doesn't mean you can't find some cool ones.

In this chapter, I look at the most popular Wii mods and hacks.

note This chapter doesn't hold your hand and take you step by step through every modification. Many of these mods are highly technical, requiring much more than a passing knowledge of electronics. You may have to understand Linux, soldering, electrical circuits, and basic programming to take on some of them.

tip Even if you're a beginner, you can perform lots of fairly simple tips and tricks without worrying about toasting your Wii. But if you don't have the expertise (or the nerve), you can have an expert do the work for you. Almost any electronic repair shop can pop a mod chip in for you.

Wii Console Hacks

You can do all kinds of things to alter the Wii, but many hacks and modifications will void your warranty. Therefore, people who are willing to dive into these procedures are not your average gamers. Still, you can find plenty of interesting ways to make the Wii (arguably) better.

note Tinkering with your Wii hardware or software may damage your Wii and will probably void your warranty. So hack and mod your Wii at your own risk.

Copy-related mods

Copy-related modifications allow the Wii to play archival copies of games. In other words, if you copy a Wii disc and then try to play the copy in your Wii, it won't work. But several mods allow you to alter your Wii so that it can play copied versions of your games. Most of these mods require opening the Wii and getting out the soldering iron, so if that makes you squeamish, read on but don't roll up your sleeves yet.

> **note**
>
> **If you assume that the only reason to mod a Wii is to copy games illegally, your assumption is wrong. Youngsters may take poor care of game discs, for example, so having backup copies to play if the originals got scratched or lost would be a huge bonus.**

CycloWiz mod chip

The CycloWiz (**Figure 10.1**) is one of the first workable mod chips for the Wii. Although it requires you to use a soldering iron and do some surgery on the Wii motherboard, it's not nearly as technical as many other mod chips.

Figure 10.1
You can pick up a CycloWiz chip for $39.95.

The CycloWiz chip offers these features:

- Fully upgradeable via DVD (meaning that the chipset firmware can be upgraded)

- Direct boot of Wii backup discs

- Direct boot to GameCube backup discs

- Direct boot of *homebrew* (homemade software) in GameCube mode

- Capable of running imported GameCube games from other regions

- Compatible with multidisc games

- Compatible with DVD-R and DVD+R media

- Easy installation (a relative claim, but true in this case)

You can get more information about the chip at the TeamCyclops Web site (www.teamcyclops.com), including highly detailed installation instructions in PDF form (**Figure 10.2**).

Figure 10.2
The CycloWiz instructions are very clear about what you must do to install the mod chip on the Wii's motherboard.

note
The current CycloWiz chip works in only two versions of the Wii: those with the Panasonic chipset numbers GC2-DMS and GC2R-D2A. If you don't find one of these chipsets when you open your Wii, you can't use the CycloWiz (yet).

Wii DVD Player

One mod that isn't readily available yet will alter the Wii's DVD drive so that it can play video DVDs, thus turning the Wii into a useful DVD player. This mod is probably going to require an upgrade of the Wii DVD player's firmware, and it's bound to be available in the coming months.

If you want to give your Wii this capability, keep checking Web sites such as http://wiihacks.blogspot.com and http://hackawii.com. When the mod for turning the Wii into a DVD player becomes available, these sites will show you how to install it.

Xeno WiiKey mod chip

Like the CycloWiz, the Xeno WiiKey (**Figure 10.3**) is easy to install; you simply place it on a certain part of the Wii motherboard and solder several points. The chip has no wires or other cumbersome items to divert your attention. Just solder it onto the few key points, and you're done.

Figure 10.3
At this writing, the Xeno WiiKey hasn't hit the market, but you can preorder it.

The Xeno's feature set includes:

- Direct boot of Wii backup discs

- Direct boot to GameCube backup discs

- Direct boot of homebrew in GameCube mode

- Capable of running imported GameCube games

- Support for all current Wii chipset versions

- Compatible with multidisc games

- Compatible with DVD-R and DVD+R media

- Easy installation

- Direct boot of Wii games from different NTSC regions

- Support for full-size (4 GB) discs for GameCube homebrew

- Recovery mode for recovery from a bad flash (meaning that if you're "flashing" the chip's memory to modify the mod chip, and the process fails, you can recover from it without losing the chip)

One key feature of the Xeno that makes it superior to the CycloWiz (at least in theory) is that it supports all current Wii motherboard chipsets. But because the Xeno isn't on the market yet, I can't test that support.

note As I write this book, a couple more mod chips have been announced, but they're still vaporware as far as I'm concerned. The only two chips that are either shipping or about to ship are the two I've mentioned, so until I see some actual hardware, I'll stick with what I know is real.

Wii software mods

Software modifications involve some aspect of the Wii console and its operating system or some part of the Wii's software. Like the hard-wired mods, most software alterations simply aren't recommended for most people—with the exception of the Duck Hunt game mod (covered in this section), which is safe and a lot of fun.

Restart the Opera browser

Several Web sites contain images that can cause the Wii's Opera Web browser to restart. This little trick can be fun to pull, but if you do this, someone could cause the browser to restart and (during the restart) load in some malicious code that could destroy your Wii. For this reason, if you come across this sort of hack, don't bother with it unless you know exactly what you're doing.

Because this type of hack is so dangerous, I'm not supplying any links here, but if you really want the links, you can find them on the hacking sites listed at the end of this chapter.

Play Duck Hunt on the Web

Remember the old Duck Hunt game, released in 1984? In this game, ducks fly up out of a grassy meadow, and you must use a light gun (a gun attached to the gaming system that can sense what's onscreen) to shoot them down.

Originally, the game was available for the Nintendo Entertainment System (NES) and in arcades. It was incredibly popular and surprisingly fun, considering its limitations.

Many people have been clamoring for Duck Hunt to be released on the Virtual Console for the Wii, because the Wii Remote can act like an old-fashioned light gun—only better. Sadly, this hasn't happened yet, but some enterprising folks have come up with a way to get the game on the Wii anyway, and I have to salute their efforts. You can play a completely authentic, enjoyable version of Duck Hunt on your Wii simply by using the Internet Channel and the Opera browser to go to a particular Web page (**Figure 10.4**).

Figure 10.4
Enter www.
nintendo-hacks.
com/duck_hunt.
swf. You have
to enter this
Web address
only once if you
make the site a
favorite.

When you pull up this Web page and get Duck Hunt
running on it (**Figure 10.5**), your Wii Remote becomes
your gun, and you can play the game right off the
bat. This hack is an amazing implementation of the
Web and the Wii together. I don't know how happy
Nintendo is about it, but it works like a charm and is
a ton of fun.

Figure 10.5
Duck Hunt
played through
a Web browser.

tip If you enjoy playing Duck Hunt on the Wii, I recommend adding the site to your Favorites area so that you don't have to enter the Web address every time you want to play it.

Mii modifications

Way back in Chapter 4, I discuss the fact that you can use both Web-based (**Figure 10.6**) and PC-based Mii editors to alter Miis in ways that you can't on the Wii itself. These programs also let you modify and store tons of Miis on your home computer, and modify and trade other people's Miis as well.

Figure 10.6
The Web-based Mii Editor in action.

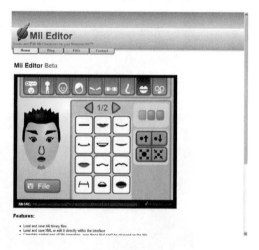

In this section, I show you the basics of transferring Miis. (I cover this process in Chapter 4 as well.) I also mention a few hacks that require altering Mii data specifications to achieve the desired results (such as getting gold pants). These techniques are not for the average user, but if you like to tinker, read on.

Transfer your Mii

first mii try.mii

Figure 10.7
A .mii file icon.

Miis are stored in little files with the .mii extension (**Figure 10.7**). You need to get these files out of your Wii Remote's storage area and download them to your computer for editing. Currently, the only way to do this is via a piece of software called MiiTransfer.

You can download MiiTransfer from various Web sites; go to http://wiihacks.blogspot.com, and search for *Miitransfer*. The software itself is tiny, taking up only 17.1 KB.

To get your Miis off your Wii Remote, you must have a Bluetooth connection on your Windows PC. (As of this writing, no Mii-transfer tools are available for the Mac.) My PC didn't have a Bluetooth system in place, so I purchased a Kensington Bluetooth USB Adapter for $59 (**Figure 10.8**); this little USB fob plugs into the USB port on the PC.

Figure 10.8
The Kensington Bluetooth USB Adapter plugs into the USB port on a PC.

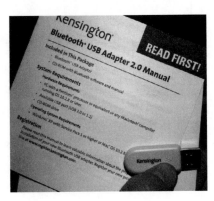

I can't take you through a step-by-step setup process, because you could have any of about a hundred Bluetooth adapters and any version of Windows, but if you follow the simple instructions that come with your adapter, setup should go swimmingly.

In my case, I put the Wii Remote next to my PC, plugged in the Bluetooth adapter, and installed the software. After that, I did a device search in the adapter software, and the Wii Remote showed up in the results list (**Figure 10.9**).

Figure 10.9
The Wii Remote shows up here as Nintendo RVL-CNT-01.

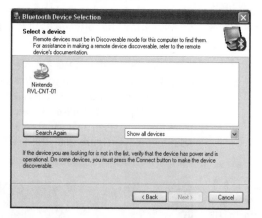

When the connection between your computer's Bluetooth adapter and the Wii Remote is established, open the Mii Transfer software folder, and double-click the MS-DOS batch file readslotALL (**Figure 10.10**). Running this little program brings up a DOS window (**Figure 10.11**) and transfers all the Miis on your remote to your PC.

Figure 10.10
Run this batch
file to get all the
Miis off your Wii
Remote (when
it's connected
to your PC via
Bluetooth).

Figure 10.11
MiiTransfer
is based on
MS-DOS.
(Remember
MS-DOS?)

Again, this process is not cut and dried; the actual
method you use depends on the versions of
Windows and MiiTransfer you're using, as well as the
type of Bluetooth adapter and driver. For detailed
(and constantly updated) directions, go to LiquidIce's
Nintendo Wii Hacks page at http://wiihacks.
blogspot.com.

note For new Mii-moving techniques, check out the Wii and
Mii hacking Web sites. It's not a stretch to imagine that
in the near future, someone will develop a slick graphical program that allows you to transfer Miis with just a
couple of clicks.

Take it easy on Mii (Surgery)

If you're serious about fooling with the real innards of Miis, check out the WiiBrew Wiki (http://wiibrew. org/index.php). This wiki provides highly detailed information about Miis in programming language (**Figure 10.12**) for those who *really* want to tinker.

Figure 10.12
The WiiBrew
Wiki is a
great place
for hard-core
programming
types.

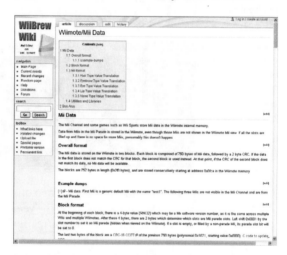

The amount of detailed information available on the Internet is truly amazing. David Hawley's blog (www.davidhawley.co.uk/blog.aspx), for example, includes a Quick Mii ID Guide for various Mii pant colors (**Figure 10.13**).

Figure 10.13

You can even find the code for Mii pant colors (in hexidecimal format) on the Web.

note

Although it may seem pointless to include this sort of information in a Pocket Guide, I'm showing it to make you aware that plenty of information on the Web can help you hack and modify your Miis to your heart's content. Editing in hex (as it's called) isn't within the scope of this book, but you can learn the basics online. It's not for everyone, but this, my friends, is the world of hacks and modifications.

Wii Laptop

Perhaps the most interesting hack of them all is the Wii Laptop (**Figure 10.14**), developed by Benjamin Heckendorn and posted by Engadget at www.engadget.com/2007/01/19/the-wii-laptop.

Figure 10.14
The Wii Laptop is one of the coolest hacks going.

According to Engadget, this laptop is an amazingly cool device with the following specifications:

- 16:9 widescreen LCD, 7-inch diagonal
- Stereo sound
- GameCube controller port
- Built-in short-range sensor bar
- Ports for the original sensor bar and AV output jacks (for use with external display)
- Built-in power supply and compartment for power cord
- Dimensions: 8.5 x 7.7 x 2 inches

You can find step-by-step instructions on how to create the Wii Laptop on Engadget's site. If you're more interested in the guy who built the Wii Laptop, check out www.benheck.com.

Wii Remote Hacks

Although hackers and modifiers usually gravitate toward the Wii console and software, the Wii Remote has inspired a ton of interesting avant-garde uses. The versatility of the Wii Remote has inspired engineers and nonengineers alike to find special uses for them.

This section looks at a few great hacks for the remote, from controlling a PC to controlling a robot.

Windows and the Wii Remote

Carl Kenner appears to be the leader in creating software that allows the Wii Remote to communicate with Windows PCs. Kenner's GlovePIE software (**Figure 10.15**) is the backbone of making the Wii Remote work in various Windows environments. *GlovePIE* stands for *Glove Programmable Input Emulator* and was designed for use with virtual-reality gloves, but Kenner has found a way to get it to work well for the Wii Remote.

Figure 10.15
GlovePIE is the backbone for Wii Remote hackers.

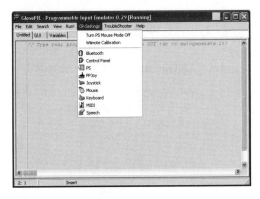

To learn more about GlovePIE and the host of possi-
bilities for those who love programming, check out
http://carl.kenner.googlepages.com/glovepie.

 note Kenner found a way to hack the Wii Remote's speaker
so that sounds can be streamed directly to the speaker
from a PC. I'm not sure what the purpose is, because the
sounds coming out of the speaker are 4-bit sounds, but
the accomplishment is interesting. Perhaps someone
out there wants "In-A-Gadda-Da-Vida" to sound like it's
coming out of a telephone underwater.

Wii Remote Drivers

Wii Remote drivers are now available for Windows users, Mac OS X
users, and even Linux users. These drivers are available at the following locations:

- Windows: GlovePIE (http://carl.kenner.googlepages.com/
  glovepie)

- Macintosh OS X: Darwiin Remote (search in the Games section of http://sourceforge.net)

- Linux: WMD (www.forthewiin.org)

Other uses for the remote

People have found so many new ways to use the
Wii Remote that making a complete list is impossible. So I decided to list a few new uses from just
the past 6 months:

- As a PC mouse input device

- As a control for a sword-wielding robot (**Figure 10.16**)

- As a control for a "smart home" (controlling heat, lights, television, security camera, and so on)

- As a laser-tag game device

- As air-drumming input devices (two remotes)

Figure 10.16
You can find some great videos on YouTube.com about the creators of this Wii Remote-controlled robot.

tip If you create a unique Wii setup, and the standard sensor bar doesn't work properly, several Web sites show you how to create homemade sensor bars.

Hack/Mod Web Sites

Hacks and mods are always changing—sometimes daily—so the best place to find information is the World Wide Web. This sidebar lists some of the best hack and modification Web sites available at this writing. (By the time you read this book, new sites may have popped up, so it behooves you to go to your favorite search engine and search for *Wii hacks* as well.)

Here's the list:

- http://wiibrew.org/index.php
- www.nintendo-hacks.com
- http://wiihacks.blogspot.com
- http://hackawii.com
- www.hackaday.com/category/wii-hacks
- http://carl.kenner.googlepages.com/glovepie_download
- www.tech-recipes.com/rx/1879/wii_hack_to_view_wii_shop
- www.wiihaveaproblem.com

Index

+/– (plus/minus) buttons
    adjusting news photos and text
        with, 70
    calibrating Wii Remote with, 116
    navigating calendar with, 133
    zooming in with, 53, 94, 126

A

accelerometers, 109
accessories
    AC cable, 179
    adding Mii, 88–89
    battery chargers, 181
    case, 178
    included with Wii, 20–21
    memory-card readers, 186
    SD Memory Cards, 184–186
    skins for Wii Remote, 174–175
    Sports Pack controller adapters, 183
    steering wheel, 184
    vertical stand, 176–177
    Wi-Fi USB connector, 43–45, 120, 182
    Wii LAN Adapter, 182–183
    wrist straps, 176
Account Activity screen, 150
activation-number box, 139
Add Wii Points screen, 140
Address Book, 97–98
AJ's Mii Editor, 105–106
audio for Wii, 33
AV cable, 24
avatars, 13, 52

B

batteries
    chargers for, 181
    installing Wii Remote, 35
Bluetooth, 111–112, 199–201
browsing. See Internet Channel; Opera
    browser

building Miis, 81–89
    adding accessories, 88–89
    eyebrows and eyes, 86–87
    hairstyles, 85–86
    head shape and skin color, 84–85
    losing and gaining weight, 84
    mouth for Miis, 88
    nose, 87
    selecting gender and name, 82–83
buttons on Wii Remote, 25
buying Wii Points Cards, 140–143

C

cables
    connecting to Internet via LAN, 46,
        121
    Nintendo component AC, 179
    Wii power, 24, 35
calendar, 132–134
calibrating Wii Remote, 114–117
cat icon, 134
channels, 47–75. *See also specific channels*
    Disc, 48–51
    displayed in main screen, 47–48
    Everybody Votes, 66, 72–73
    Forecast, 67–68
    illustrated, 14, 47
    Internet, 74–75
    Mii, 51–55
    navigation arrows for, 49
    News, 69–71
    Photo, 55–64
    standard, 15
    updates for, 15
    Wii Shop, 65–67
Cheat button, 64
Classic Controller, 9
connecting to Internet, 39–46
    encrypted wireless networks, 42–43
    setting up WiiConnect24, 122–123
    using existing unencrypted wireless
        networks, 39–41
    using Nintendo Wi-Fi USB Connector,
        43–45, 120
    via LAN cable, 46, 121
Connector Registration Tool, 44–45
connectors, 23

console
    decorative skins for Wii, 175
    Intec Wii Pro Gamer's case for, 178
    vertical stand for, 176–177
content, 154–155
controller sockets, 23, 24
controllers. *See also* Wii Remote
    checking game requirements for, 154
    Classic Controller, 9
    GameCube, 10–11, 177
    Nunchuk, 8
    Wii Sports Pack controller adapters, 183
copy-related mods, 191–195
    CycloWiz mod chip, 191–193
    reasons for, 191
    Xeno WiiKey mod chip, 193–194
CPU (central processing unit), 30–31
cursor
    disappears from TV screen, 113
    flickering, 114–117
CycloWiz mod chip, 191–193

D

decorative Wii console skins, 175
Details screen, 146
Disc Channel, 48–51
    about, 14
    display when disc inserted, 50
    illustrated, 15
    screen before inserting disc, 48–49
disc drive, 22, 31
discs
    ejecting and inserting, 50–51
    Wii Sports, 27–28
Doodle options, 63
Download Confirmation screen, 147
Download Software screen, 143, 147
downloading
    new Internet Channel version, 149
    Virtual Console games, 144–148
drivers for Wii Remote, 206
Duck Hunt, 196–198

E

editing. *See also* PC-based editors;
        Web-based editors
    Miis outside Wii, 90, 91, 100–106
    slideshow settings, 59–60

Eject button, 22, 50
email, 131
encrypted wireless networks, 42–43
entering Web site address, 126
ESRB (Entertainment Software Rating
        Board) rating system, 130, 157
Etsy.com, 151
Everybody Votes Channel
        availability of, 66
        illustrated, 72, 73
        registering Miis to vote, 72
eyebrows and eyes, 86–87

F

favorites
        saving Duck Hunt as Web, 197, 198
        Web site, 75, 124–125
flash memory, 31, 32
Flash Player, 101
force feedback of Wii Remote, 110
Forecast Channel, 67–68
Fun! screen options, 61–64
        Doodle, 63
        Mood, 62
        Puzzle, 64

G

game ratings
        checking before game purchase, 155
        ESRB system for, 130, 157
        setting levels of, 129–130
        top Web sites for, 156
        updated Virtual Console, 165
GameCube
        Classic Controller for, 9
        compatibility with Wii, 4, 10–11,
                164, 169
        introduction of, 3
        Lego Star Wars II: The Original
                Trilogy for, 170–171
        Luigi's Mansion for, 171
        memory-card slots on Wii for, 23,
                24, 32
        starting from Disc Channel, 14
        Super Smash Bros. Melee for, 172
        toppling Wii when using
                controllers, 177
        Wii controller sockets for, 23, 24

games
        best Wii, 157–163
        enjoyment using Wii, 17–18
        GT Pro Series, 158
        history of Nintendo, 2–3
        Legend of Zelda: Twilight Princess, 159
        Lego Star Wars II: The Original
                Trilogy, 170–171
        Luigi's Mansion, 171
        Madden NFL 07, 160
        online rating information for, 155–156
        operations guides for Virtual
                Console, 169
        Rayman Raving Rabbids, 161–162
        Red Steel, 162
        selecting Wii, 154–155
        Super Mario 64, 166
        Super Mario World, 167
        Super Smash Bros. Melee, 172
        ToeJam & Earl, 168
        Wario Ware: Smooth Moves, 163
        Wii's backward compatibility, 11, 164
gender for Miis, 82
Globe feature, 68
globe view with News Channel, 71
GlovePIE software mods for Wii Remote,
        205–206
GPU (graphics processing unit), 30–31
grabbing Miis, 94–95
GT Pro Series, 158

H

hacks. See mods and hacks
hairstyles, 85–86
head shape for Miis, 84–85
help
        finding tips via cat icon, 134
        Internet Channel button for, 124, 127

I

icons
        cat, 134
        .mii file, 199
        whistle, 53
identifying Miis, 93
infrared sensing with Wii Remote, 112–113
inserting discs, 50–51
installing CycloWiz mod chip, 192

Intec G5615 Wii vertical stand, 176–177
Intec Wii Pro Gamer's case, 178
interface tour, 14–16. *See also* screens
interference with infrared technology, 113
Internet button (Wii System Settings 2 screen), 40
Internet Channel, 74–75
    downloading new version, 149
    emailing via Opera browser, 131
    Favorites area of, 124–125
    parental controls, 127–130
    restricting use of, 130
    shopping from, 151
    start page for, 124
    as Web browser, 74
Internet connections. *See* connecting to Internet

K

Ken Burns Effect, 59, 60
Kensington Bluetooth USB Adapter, 199

L

LAN
    Internet connections using, 46, 121
    Nintendo Wii LAN Adapter, 182–183
Legend of Zelda, The: Twilight Princess, 159
Lego Star Wars II: The Original Trilogy, 170–171
Luigi's Mansion, 171

M

Madden NFL 07, 160
Mail button, 16
main screen, 47–48
managing Miis, 93–100
    arranging Miis, 95
    identifying Miis, 93
    picking up Miis, 94–95
    sending Mii to friend, 96–97
    transferring Miis, 98–100
    zooming in on Mii Plaza, 53, 93–94
memory. *See also* SD Memory Cards
    flash, 31
    storage for Wii Remote, 32
memory-card readers, 185–186
memory-card slots, 23, 24, 32

memos, 132
Mii Channel, 51–55. *See also* Miis
    about, 51–52
    avatars, 52
    creating Miis in, 12–13, 54–55
    Mii Parade, 53–54
    Mii Plaza, 52–53
    traveling Miis, 52, 83, 90
Mii Editor, 101–102, 198
Mii modifications, 198–203
    checking WiiBrew Wiki for, 202
    code for pant colors, 202–203
Mii Parade, 53–54
Mii Plaza
    about, 52–53
    command buttons for, 91–92
    navigating, 91–92
    zooming on Mii Plaza, 53, 93–94
Miis, 77–106. *See also* building Miis
    about, 12
    arranging, 95
    building from scratch, 81–89
    creating, 54–55
    custom pant colors for, 202–203
    editing, 90, 100–106
    grabbing, 94–95
    identifying, 93
    limits on editing, 90, 91
    mingling, 83
    navigating Mii Plaza, 91–92
    options for creating, 80–81
    pronunciation of, 77
    registering to vote, 72
    role of, 78–79
    sending to friend, 96–97
    transferring, 98–100, 199–201
    traveling, 52, 83, 90
    zooming in on Mii Plaza, 53, 93–94
MiiTransfer, 199–201
mingling, 83
minus button. *See* plus/minus (+/–) buttons
modifications. *See* mods and hacks
mods and hacks, 189–208. *See also* copy-related mods; Mii modifications; software mods
    about, 189–190
    cautions about, 190

copy-related, 191–195
GlovePIE software mods for Wii
    Remote, 205–206
innovative uses for Wii Remote,
    206–207
Mii modifications, 198–203
playing video DVDs on Wii, 193
sensor bar mods, 207
software mods, 195–199
Web sites for more, 208
Wii Laptop, 204
Xeno WiiKey mod chip, 193–194
Mood options, 62
mouth for Miis, 88
MP3 files
    playing with slideshow, 60–61
    transferring to and from Wii, 187

N

naming Miis, 82–83
navigating
    Mii Plaza, 91–92
    through channels, 49
New Mii button, 81
News Channel, 69–71
    globe view with, 71
    highlighting text, 70
    illustrated, 69
    restricting use of, 130
    viewing news items, 69–70
nicknames, 82–83
Nintendo
    games made by, 2–3
    Wi-Fi USB Connector, 43–45, 120, 182
    Wii LAN Adapter, 182–183
Nintendo Wii Hacks Web page, 201
nose for Miis, 87
Nunchuk, 8, 26, 109

O

One Time Mode setup, 36–37
Opera browser
    email via, 131
    future pricing of, 66, 74
    mods restarting, 195
    playing Duck Hunt from, 196–198
    surfing Web from Wii, 124–127

operations guides for Virtual Console
    games, 169
option buttons for slideshow, 59

P

parental controls, 127–130
Parental Controls button (Wii System
    Settings 2 screen), 128
passwords
    protecting Wii services with, 128
    using for encrypted wireless
        networks, 42–43
PC-based editors, 104–106
    AJ's Mii Editor, 105–106
    Wii - M!! Editor, 104–105
Photo Channel, 55–64
    Fun! screen options, 61–64
    inserting photos with SD card,
        56–57, 187
    slideshows, 58–61
    start screen for, 56
    using SD Memory Card with, 55–56
    viewing individual photos on, 58
photos inserted from SD Memory Cards,
    56–57, 187
PIN (personal identification number),
    129–130
playing video DVDs on Wii, 193
plus/minus (+/−) buttons
    adjusting news photos and text
        with, 70
    calibrating Wii Remote with, 116
    navigating calendar with, 133
    zooming in with, 53, 94, 126
ports, 23, 33
power cable, 24, 35
processors for Wii, 30–31
progressive-scan output, 179–180
purchasing Virtual Console games,
    144–148
Puzzle options, 64

R

Rayman Raving Rabbids, 161–162
red pencil for news items, 70
Red Steel, 162
redeeming Wii Points Cards, 138–140
reliability of Wii Shop Channel, 136

restricting mail and content
    exchanged, 130
rumble, 110, 114

S

saving
    Duck Hunt as Web favorite, 197, 198
    Miis on Wii Remote, 99
screens. *See also* Fun! screen options; Wii
    System Settings 2 screen
    Account Activity, 150
    Add Wii Points, 140
    channels on main, 47–48
    Details, 146
    Download Confirmation, 147
    Download Software, 143, 147
    Photo Channel start, 56
    Slide-Show Settings, 59
    start page for Internet Channel, 124
    System Settings, 122
    Wii Points Purchase, 141–142
    Wii Points Purchase Confirmation, 143
    Wii Settings, 16
SD Memory Cards, 31, 32
    about, 184–185
    card readers for, 185–186
    inserting photos from, 56–57, 187
    photo transfers to Wii with, 55
    slot for, 22, 24, 32
    transferring music to and from Wii
        with, 187
Sensitivity button, 115
sensor bar
    about, 6
    calibrating sensitivity of, 115–117
    infrared sensing of, 112–113
    mods for, 207
Sensor Bar button (Wii System Settings 2
    screen), 115
sensor bar port, 23, 33
setting up Wii, 34–46. *See also* connecting
    to Internet
    Internet connection, 39–46
    steps for, 34–35
    Wii Remote setup steps, 36–38
Settings button, 16
shopping. *See also* Wii Points Cards; Wii
    Shop Channel

Internet Channel, 151
reliability of Wii Shop Channel, 136
Show Games from One Game System
    button, 145
skin color for Miis, 84
skins
    console, 175
    Wii Remote, 174–175
Slide-Show Settings screen, 59
slideshows, 58–61
    adding music to, 60–61
    option buttons for, 59
software
    downloading, 147
    provided in box, 27–28
software mods, 195–198
    GlovePIE mods for Wii Remote,
        205–206
    playing Duck Hunt on Web, 196–198
    restarting Opera browser, 195
sound
    adjusting settings for, 114
    from Wii Remote, 110
speaker on Wii Remote
    adjusting volume of, 114
    illustrated, 108
    sound from, 110
    streaming sound from PC to, 206
stands for Wii, 26–27
steering wheel, 184
strategy guides, 155
Super Mario 64, 166
Super Mario World, 167
Super Smash Bros. Melee, 172
surfing Web from Wii, 74, 124–127
Sync button, 22, 24
synchronizing
    new remote, 38–39
    Wii Remote for One Time setup, 36–37

T

television
    cursor disappears from screen, 113
    flickering cursor on, 114–117
    progressive scan in 480p mode,
        179–180
tips, 134
ToeJam & Earl, 168

transferring Miis, 98–100, 199–201
traveling Miis, 52, 83, 90

U

Ubisoft Wii steering wheel, 184
unexpected onscreen behavior, 114–117
updates, channel, 15

V

vertical stand, 176–177
video for Wii, 33
video processors, 31
viewing
    individual photos, 58
    news items, 69–70
Virtual Console
    about, 66–67
    Classic controller with, 9
    compatibility with Wii, 164
    GameCube controllers with, 11
    illustrated, 11, 165
    operations guides for games on, 169
    purchasing and downloading games
        for, 144–148
    Super Mario 64, 166
    Super Mario World, 167
    ToeJam & Earl, 168
voting, 72, 78–79

W

Wario Ware: Smooth Moves, 163
weather updates, 121
Web sites
    adding to favorites, 75, 124–125, 197,
        198
    entering address for, 126
    finding mods and hacks, 208
    Nintendo Wii Hacks, 201
    online game reviews, 155–156
    playing Duck Hunt from, 196–198
    surfing, 74, 124–127
Web-based editors, 100–103
    Mii Editor, 101–102, 198
    Wii-volution, 103
weight for Miis, 84
WEP (Wired Equivalent Privacy), 43
whistle icon, 53

Wii. *See also* setting up Wii
    accessories included with, 20–21
    audio and video for, 33
    cables for, 24
    calendar, 132–134
    cautions modifying, 190
    compatibility with earlier games,
        11, 164
    controller sockets, 23, 24
    controllers for, 4–11
    creating memos with, 132
    decorative skins for console, 175
    enjoyment using, 17–18
    flash memory and storage for, 31–32
    GameCube compatibility with, 4,
        10–11, 164, 169
    illustrated, 22–23
    interface tour of, 14–16
    Internet connectivity with, 120–123
    introduction of, 3, 17
    mailing other Wii users from, 131
    memory-card slots, 23, 24, 32
    Nunchuk, 8, 26
    password-protecting services in, 128
    playing video DVDs on, 193
    ports, 23, 33
    processors for, 30–31
    progressive-scan output for, 179–180
    selecting games for, 154–155
    sensor bar, 6, 112–113
    software provided for, 27–28
    stands for, 26–27
    surfing Web from, 74, 124–127
    Virtual Console for, 11
    Wii Remote, 25
Wii Address Book, 97–98
Wii Laptop, 204
Wii - M!! Editor, 104–105
Wii Number, 97–98
Wii Points, 137, 148
Wii Points Cards, 137–143
    Activation Number, 139
    buying, 140–143
    checking account activity for, 150
    redeeming, 138–140
    Wii Points and, 137, 148
Wii Points Purchase Confirmation
    screen, 143

Wii Points Purchase screen, 141–142
Wii Remote, 4–7, 108–117
　about, 4–7, 25
　accelerometers for, 109
　adjusting settings for, 114
　Bluetooth technology and, 111–112
　calibrating, 114–117
　charging batteries for, 181
　Doodle options using, 63
　drivers for, 206
　force feedback of, 110
　GlovePIE software mods for, 205–206
　illustrated, 5, 25, 108
　infrared sensing with, 112–113
　innovative uses for, 206–207
　installing batteries for, 35
　memory storage for, 32
　Nunchuk add-on controller, 8, 26
　One Time Mode setup, 36–37
　sensor bar for, 6, 112–113
　setting up, 36–38
　skins for, 174–175
　sound from, 110, 114
　Standard Mode setup, 37–38
　synchronizing new, 38–39
　transferring Miis to, 98–100
　using Classic Controller with, 9
　Wii Sports Pack controller adapters
　　for, 183
　wrist strap for, 7, 176
Wii Remote Settings option, 36–37
Wii Settings screen, 16
Wii Shop Channel, 135–151
　about, 11, 65
　checking account activity, 150
　illustrated, 135
　making Virtual Console purchases,
　　144–148
　reliability of, 136
　restricting use of, 130
　using Wii Points Cards, 137–143
　Virtual Console, 66–67
　Wii Ware, 65–66, 149–150
Wii Sports disc, 27–28
Wii Sports Pack controller adapters, 183
Wii System Settings 2 screen
　Internet button, 40
　Parental Controls button, 128
　Sensor Bar button on, 115
　setting up WiiConnect24, 122–123
Wii Ware, 65–66, 149–150
WiiBrew Wiki, 202
WiiConnect24
　about, 67, 121–122
　activating to receive traveling Miis, 90
　restricting mail and content
　　exchanged via, 130
　setting up, 122–123
Wiimote. See Wii Remote
Wii-volution, 103
Wireless Connection button, 41
wireless networks
　communication ranges for devices,
　　112, 113
　encrypted, 42–43
　unencrypted, 39–41
wrist straps, 7, 176

X
Xeno WiiKey mod chip, 193–194

Z
Zoom –/ Zoom + options, 57
zooming in/out, 53, 94, 126